EDIBLE DALLAS & FORT WORTH: THE COOKBOOK

EDIBLE DALLAS & FORT WORTH: THE COOKBOOK

EDITED BY TERRI TAYLOR

PHOTOGRAPHS BY CAROLE TOPALIAN

STERLING EPICURE
New York

STERLING EPICURE
New York

An Imprint of Sterling Publishing
387 Park Avenue South
New York, NY 10016

ISBN 978-1-4027-8556-6

Library of Congress Cataloging-in-Publication Data

Edible Dallas & Fort Worth : the cookbook / edited by Terri Taylor ; photographs by Carole Topalian.
      pages cm
   ISBN 978-1-4027-8556-6 (hardback)
 1. Cooking, American--Southwestern style. 2. Cooking--Texas--Dallas. 3. Cooking--Texas--Fort Worth. I. Taylor, Terri. II. Title:
Edible Dallas and Fort Worth : the cookbook.
   TX715.2.S69E35 2012
   641.59764'2812--dc23
                              2012002861

Distributed in Canada by Sterling Publishing
c/o Canadian Manda Group, 165 Dufferin Street
Toronto, Ontario, Canada M6K 3H6

For information about custom editions, special sales, and premium and corporate purchases,
please contact Sterling Special Sales at 800-805-5489 or specialsales@sterlingpublishing.com.

Manufactured in Canada

2 4 6 8 10 9 7 5 3 1

www.sterlingpublishing.com

CONTENTS

FOREWORD

What you hold in your hand is the third in a series of community cookbooks created by Edible Communities—a network of regional food magazines across the United States and Canada.

It's thoroughly cutting edge—gleaned from the kitchens and pantries of the chefs, drink makers, food artisans, home cooks, caterers, ranchers, gardeners, and avid eaters who make up today's Dallas and Fort Worth food communities.

But this cookbook is also an old soul—kin to the community cookbooks that have been published by churches, schools, and other collections of like-minded individuals throughout North America for centuries.

Communities crave cookbooks. In fact, they need them: to document and codify food traditions; to remind us of what's in season; and to chronicle and celebrate the people in our communities who feed and sustain us.

No matter if today's cookbook is organized by urban CSA members or the teachers behind an Edible schoolyard project, or if recipes once gathered on ruled cards are now crowd-sourced on email: the mission remains the same.

This same mission was part inspiration for *Edible Ojai*, the first Edible magazine, launched in 2002. The simple and revolutionary idea—which has now manifested in more than 70 Edible magazines in big cities, little towns, and everywhere in between— was that telling the story behind our food would encourage us all to eat better, restore our landscape, support our neighbors, and generally make food and drink experiences a bigger, richer part of our collective lives.

Beginning with Brooklyn, and following with Seattle, Dallas–Fort Worth, the Twin Cities, and beyond, Edible Communities, the network of local food magazines in distinct culinary regions throughout the United States and Canada, will publish a series of cookbooks that celebrate those areas where Edible magazines exist. In keeping with the pages of local Edible magazines, these cookbooks invite 100 or so people from the various food communities to submit original recipes that tell something about their place and their place in it.

This particular installation is packed with gussied-up Texas favorites, like bacon- and jalapeño-stuffed quail breasts, chili con carne, and crispy chicken with blue corn grits. A world-class chef dishes up his venison meatball sliders, a pioneer in artisan cheese making offers her beet and feta salad recipe, and a community gardener assembles a fried green tomato sandwich. A farmer guarantees that we're going to love her family's sweet potato casserole, and a rancher reveals the tricks of slow-cooking the perfect chuck roast. Within these pages, Dallas and Fort Worth's top chefs and food writers share not only their treasured recipes, but also the names of favorite farms, ranches, and food purveyors. The aim here is to introduce the region's deep-rooted food traditions and to acknowledge the hard-working folks who produce the food that fuels that culture.

Wherever you may be, please consider this cookbook inspiration to get to know the people who feed you.

—*Tracey Ryder, co-founder, Edible Communities, Inc.; Nanci Taylor, Publisher, and Terri Taylor, Editor,* Edible Dallas & Fort Worth

Est. DALLAS 1941

FARMERS MARKET

INTRODUCTION

Texas cuisine—there's nothing quite like it, whether it's chili con carne dished up over a campfire or chilled watermelon soup served on a sweltering summer's day. The recipes in this cookbook represent our unique part of the world, and the foods that we grow. These are our comfort foods, the foods of our childhood, our special occasion foods, the foods that we crave. The task of stitching together an intimate cookbook representative of two major cities and over 6.5 million North Texans presented an interesting challenge. For anyone who hasn't heard: there's a friendly rivalry between Dallas and her sister city Fort Worth.

Fort Worth, a.k.a. Cowtown, embraces its Western roots and is steeped in history. The Chisholm Trail brought herds of cattle and cowboys here before the turn of the 20th century. Fort Worth's early success was a result of the cattle trade and a world that revolved around the stockyards. Today, Fort Worth has a casual, down-home vibe, but past the jeans and boots, there's more than what meets the eye. Fort Worth has sophisticated, world-class museums, and its restaurants, particularly those featuring farm to table fare, have been attracting national attention. There's an abundance of local beef and wild Texas game on its menus, but savvy chefs are also buying locally grown veggies. Even cowboys like carrots these days.

Dallas, Cowtown's slick sister to the east, is a city of commerce and fashion, always moving forward, rarely looking back. Dallas's food scene has long been a magnet for hip new restaurants and culinary trendsetters. Flash back to the 1980s, when restaurants and restaurant goers began embracing the New American cuisine, which had its beginnings in California. That's when iconic chefs Stephan Pyles and Dean Fearing began experimenting with edible things in their own backyards. Along with others, they created Southwestern cuisine, and suddenly North Texas was a destination on the New American culinary map.

Dallas cheese maker Paula Lambert, one of the few Americans handcrafting cheese in those days, remembers being inspired when she learned of the indigenous herbs and local chiles that Pyles and Fearing were using. She took their lead, and thirty years later she's still incorporating a variety of herbs and local ingredients into her cheeses. During the growing season, there are now more than thirty farmers' markets in and around the Dallas–Fort Worth Metroplex.

North Texas sits at the crossroads of several strong culinary traditions. To the east of Dallas, there are rolling pastures, vineyards, a string of lakes, and piney woods. Kitchens are filled with the aromas of the South, of grits and collard greens, of fried green tomatoes and okra in browned butter, of blackberry-peach cobbler and bourbon-doused bread pudding. Cajun and Creole seasonings also influence local tables. In the summer, the Gulf breezes remind folks that the coast and a fresh catch of shrimp or fish are only a few hours away.

To the west of Fort Worth, there are wide-open skies over prairies and plains. This is cattle country, where the West begins. Like the chuck wagon cooks of our past, modern chefs roast meats and wild game over mesquite embers. The indigenous peppers and herbs, used for hundreds of years by Native Americans, still add fire and flavor to our regional dishes. Our cuisine is a composite influenced by all who laid claim to this territory.

I hope this cookbook and its 100 plus recipes give you some insight into our North Texas foodways. Texans are fiercely proud of their heritage and we're mighty proud of our food. Hopefully, some of these recipes will become favorites of yours too.

—*Terri Taylor*

CHAPTER 1

STARTERS

In spite of our region's warm climate, North Texans are an outdoorsy bunch who love tailgate dining and backyard get-togethers. We've included some of our very favorite appetizers, like Texas Caviar and Gulf Fish Ceviche, to be savored, of course, with a cold local beer or a glass of chilled Texas Viognier. When the summer heat index is topping the charts, a light but well-endowed salad is more than a starter; it's the star of the show, and there are some stunners on the following pages. We cook with hot chiles and chilly watermelons, cucumbers and citrus, in equal amounts. And we love our Texas goat cheese. You'll find an abundance of tangy white chèvre in many of these pre-entrée delights.

BABY BIBB AND SHAVED RADISHES WITH APPLEWOOD-SMOKED BACON AND GREEN GODDESS DRESSING

From Molly McCook, Ellerbe Fine Foods, Fort Worth

Located in a renovated 1920s gas station, Ellerbe Fine Foods exudes southern charm: fresh flowers, light-filled windows, vintage decor. The Ellerbe menu is a testimony to chef Molly McCook's devotion to area farmers. There are Scott Farm beets, B & G Garden's haricots verts, Carter Farms potatoes, Cox Farm arugula, and Parker County peaches. "I try to get as much as possible from the market," says McCook. "We have a story behind every vegetable on the plate . . . and you feel the love of the farmer." In the lobby alcove, there are shelves of boutique wines, local jellies, and other artisanal food products for sale.

McCook and co-owner/general manager Richard King are natives of Shreveport, Louisiana. McCook received her farm-to-table training working with Amaryll Schwertner in San Francisco and as sous-chef with Suzanne Goin in Los Angeles. In this recipe, McCook tosses local Bibb lettuce in creamy green goddess dressing and tops it with crumbled smoked bacon and wafer-thin radishes.

Edible Tip

Any remaining dressing can be stored in the refrigerator, covered, for up to 1 week.

FOR THE DRESSING:
2 CUPS MAYONNAISE
LEAVES FROM 1 BUNCH FRESH FLAT-LEAF PARSLEY
LEAVES FROM 3–4 SPRIGS FRESH TARRAGON
1 BUNCH GREEN ONIONS (GREEN PARTS ONLY)
1 SHALLOT, MINCED
2 TSP SALT
½ TSP FRESHLY GROUND BLACK PEPPER
1 CLOVE GARLIC, GRATED WITH A MICROPLANE
¼ CUP CHAMPAGNE VINEGAR
1 TBSP DRY MUSTARD
JUICE AND ZEST OF 1 LEMON
¾ CUP CRÈME FRAÎCHE
¼ CUP BUTTERMILK

FOR THE SALAD:
3 HEADS BABY BIBB LETTUCE, LEAVES SEPARATED, WASHED, AND DRIED
6 LARGE RADISHES, CUT WITH A MANDOLINE OR SLICED AS THIN AS POSSIBLE
4 SLICES APPLEWOOD-SMOKED BACON, COOKED UNTIL CRISP AND CRUMBLED

Serves 6

MAKE THE DRESSING:

1 In a blender on medium speed, puree the mayonnaise, parsley, tarragon, and green onions until the mayonnaise has a vibrant green color and the herbs are well blended. Using just a few pulses, blend in the shallot, salt, pepper, garlic, vinegar, mustard, and lemon juice and zest. On the blender's lowest speed, blend in the crème fraîche and buttermilk. Adjust the seasonings to taste.

ASSEMBLE THE SALAD:

2 In a large bowl, toss the lettuce and dressing together to coat; use as much of the dressing as you like. Divide the dressed lettuce among 6 plates, arranging the leaves like cups. Top the salads with the shaved radishes and crumbled bacon.

TEXAS CAVIAR

From Kelly Yandell,
TheMeaningofPie.com

There are all kinds of names for (and varieties of) that local food we all call black-eyed peas. In fact, they are cowpeas, which are beans. There are many regional cousins, such as crowders, colored-eyes, and creamers, and the varietal names are wonderful: Mississippi Silverbrown, Blue Goose, Texas Big Boy, and Dixie Queen, to name only a few. Cowpeas are an exceptional Texas crop because they are drought tolerant and thrive in harsh conditions. Texas Caviar is a classic Texas dish. This version by food writer Kelly Yandell packs a lot of flavor into the humble little dip, and it's easy, inexpensive, and healthy. Even if you choose to make this with canned black-eyed peas when fresh are not in season, try the homemade vinaigrette. It makes a huge difference, and you'll be rewarded with a fresher, more piquant dip.

Edible Tips

◆ This is best made a day, or at least several hours, in advance so that the flavors can blend together nicely. The caviar will keep in the refrigerator for several days. You may strain off some of the vinaigrette before serving, but be gentle because it is really tasty and you don't want to lose too much.

◆ You can substitute 2 (15-ounce) cans drained black-eyed peas for the fresh peas, if necessary.

FOR THE PEAS:
3 CUPS FRESH BLACK-EYED PEAS
½ MEDIUM ONION, HALVED
1 SLICE THICK-CUT BACON
1 (14 OZ) CAN LOW-SODIUM
    CHICKEN BROTH

FOR THE VINAIGRETTE:
½ CUP EXTRA-VIRGIN OLIVE OIL
¼ CUP CHAMPAGNE VINEGAR
1½ TSP LIGHT BROWN SUGAR
½ TSP GROUND CUMIN
¼ TSP CAYENNE

FOR THE DIP:
1 RED BELL PEPPER, SEEDED AND
    CUT INTO SMALL DICE

1 LARGE JALAPEÑO CHILE, MINCED
1 CLOVE GARLIC, MINCED
3 GREEN ONIONS (WHITE AND
    LIGHT GREEN PARTS ONLY),
    THINLY SLICED
10–15 GRAPE TOMATOES, ROUGHLY
    CHOPPED
1 TSP MINCED FRESH OREGANO
1 TSP CHOPPED FRESH PARSLEY
SALT
FRESHLY GROUND BLACK PEPPER

FOR SERVING:
TORTILLA CHIPS

Serves 8

COOK THE PEAS:
1 Place the black-eyed peas, onion, bacon, and broth in a medium saucepan. Add enough water to cover the peas. Simmer over medium heat, uncovered, until the peas are cooked to your liking, 25–30 minutes. Strain the peas into a colander. Discard the onion and bacon.

MAKE THE VINAIGRETTE:
2 Place the olive oil, vinegar, brown sugar, cumin, and cayenne in a lidded jar and shake until the mixture is emulsified.

ASSEMBLE THE DIP:
3 Place the cooked peas, red pepper, jalapeño, garlic, green onions, tomatoes, oregano, and parsley in a medium bowl. Pour the vinaigrette over the ingredients and combine well. Season as needed with salt and pepper. Cover the dish with plastic wrap and refrigerate until you are ready to serve. Serve with tortilla chips.

GRILLED WATERMELON SALAD

From Leslie Finical Halleck, North Haven Gardens, Dallas

Watermelon? Grilled? Yes, and it's really good. And easy too. This unusual summer salad is meatless, yet meaty. When rindless watermelon squares are grilled, they take on a texture and density similar to that of a tuna steak (with none of the fishiness, of course). After grilling, the caramelized squares are stacked with layers of peppery arugula, generous sprinkles of goat cheese, and a sweet drizzle of balsamic reduction. If you're already firing up the grill for your favorite meat, try this fun and quirky accompaniment. It's an impressive forkful and quite the conversation starter. Grilled watermelon . . . Really?

Edible Tips

♦ Baby spinach may be substituted for the arugula.
♦ Because of the potent fumes, be sure to open a kitchen window or turn on the stove's fan while heating the vinegar.
♦ Cutting the blocks to a 1-inch thickness will give the melon a meatier texture. If you want a lighter salad, you can cut the blocks thinner.

½ SMALL SEEDLESS WATERMELON
 (ABOUT 5 LB)
1 CUP BALSAMIC VINEGAR
1 CUP EXTRA-VIRGIN OLIVE OIL
SALT

2–3 CUPS ARUGULA
1½ CUPS CRUMBLED GOAT CHEESE
FRESHLY GROUND BLACK PEPPER

Serves 4

1 Heat the grill to very hot (the hotter the grill, the better the grill marks on the watermelon; you can also use an indoor grill pan on your stove top over high heat).

2 While the grill is heating, cut away the rind so that you are left with a large rindless block of watermelon. Cut the block into 1-inch-thick slices; then cut each slice into 3-inch squares. For 4 salads, you will need 8 squares.

3 In a small saucepan, simmer the vinegar over medium heat until reduced by half, about 5 minutes. It should have a thick, syrupy consistency. Let it cool before serving.

4 Brush or drizzle each side of the watermelon blocks with a thin coat of olive oil; then place on the hot grill for approximately 2 minutes on each side. Remove from the grill and season with a little salt.

5 Place about ¼ cup of arugula on each of 4 salad plates. On top of the greens, place one slice of grilled watermelon, sprinkle with one-eighth of the goat cheese, and drizzle with a bit of the balsamic reduction. On top of that stack, add another ¼ cup of greens, then a second slice of watermelon, and sprinkle with the remaining goat cheese. Drizzle a bit more balsamic reduction over the whole salad, and add a light drizzle of olive oil. Finish with a pinch of black pepper on top.

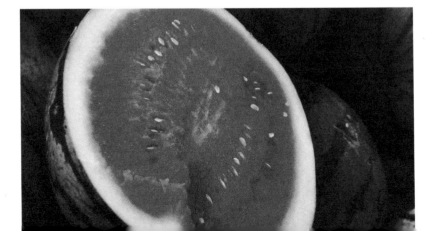

ROCKY'S MINER'S LETTUCE SALAD WITH SHERRY VINAIGRETTE DRESSING

From Chad Houser and Janice Provost, Parigi, Dallas

Miner's lettuce supposedly derived its name from the California miners who foraged and ate this native plant, rich in vitamins A and C, to ward off scurvy during the gold rush days. The plant's tender, succulent, almost heart-shaped leaf has a mild and pleasantly fresh taste. On the seasonal menu at Parigi, a bistro in Dallas's Oak Lawn neighborhood, chefs Chad Houser and Janice Provost pay homage to the farmers who inspire their creations. Houser's spring salad features miner's lettuce grown at Tassione Farms near Stephenville. In their hydroponic greenhouses, Rocky and Celeste Tassione produce a year-round supply of organic baby lettuces, microgreens, tomatoes, and herbs for many of the area's most savvy restaurants. In this recipe, miner's lettuce is tossed in a sherry vinaigrette, then topped with lightly fried spring leeks, bits of bacon, and festive grapes pickled in Champagne vinegar. Sprinkled over each serving are grated shavings of Bosque Blue, an aged, blue-veined cheese named after the Bosque River, which runs near Veldhuizen Family Farm.

Edible Tip

If miner's lettuce isn't available, use baby spinach or spring mix.

FOR THE PICKLED GRAPES:
4 SPRIGS FRESH TARRAGON
1½ CUPS CHAMPAGNE VINEGAR
1 TBSP SUGAR
1½ TSP PICKLING SALT
4 CUPS RED GRAPES

FOR THE SHERRY VINAIGRETTE:
1 TSP CHOPPED GARLIC
¼ CUP SHERRY VINEGAR
1 TBSP DIJON MUSTARD
¾ CUP EXTRA-VIRGIN OLIVE OIL (TEXAS OLIVE RANCH PREFERRED)
SALT
FRESHLY GROUND BLACK PEPPER

FOR THE FRIED LEEKS:
CANOLA OIL FOR FRYING
2 SPRING LEEKS (WHITE PART ONLY), WASHED THOROUGHLY, DRIED, AND SLICED INTO ¼-INCH RINGS
½ CUP FLOUR SEASONED WITH SALT AND PEPPER FOR DREDGING

FOR THE SALAD:
6 CUPS TASSIONE FARMS MINER'S LETTUCE, WASHED AND SPUN DRY
½ CUP BACON, COOKED UNTIL CRISP AND CHOPPED
5 OZ VELDHUIZEN'S BOSQUE BLUE CHEESE, FROZEN

Serves 4

MAKE THE PICKLED GRAPES:
1 Combine the tarragon, vinegar, sugar, pickling salt, and ½ cup water in a small saucepan and bring to a boil. Let cool slightly and pour over the grapes in a heatproof bowl. Let the grapes sit covered in the refrigerator at least 3 hours before serving, or overnight for best results.

MAKE THE SHERRY VINAIGRETTE:
2 Whisk the garlic, vinegar, mustard, olive oil, salt, and pepper together in a large bowl.

MAKE THE FRIED LEEKS:
3 Heat the oil in a skillet to 350°F. Dip the leek rings in the seasoned flour and lightly coat. Shake off any excess flour. Place the leeks in the hot oil and fry until golden brown. Remove with a slotted spoon and drain on a paper towel. Set aside.

ASSEMBLE THE SALAD:
4 Toss the lettuce with the vinaigrette and divide among 4 salad plates. Top each salad with a sprinkling of bacon, the grapes, and the leeks. Grate the frozen blue cheese over the salad.

J.T. LEMLEY

Lemley's Produce and Plant Farm, Canton

For thirty-five years, J.T. Lemley has been selling his legendary tomatoes and so much more at the Dallas Farmers Market. That's half of the market's seventy-year existence. It's a one-hour drive from farm to market, and J.T. makes it several times a week for the loyal following of chefs and home cooks who depend on his weekly produce.

His farm is located near the East Texas town of Canton. There's a small retail store on the edge of the property where J.T. sells homemade peach ice cream and baskets of fresh produce in the summer and starter plants from his greenhouse in the spring. The store walls are decorated with decades of photos and framed magazine articles about J.T. and his wife, Carolyn, who was also a familiar face at the Dallas Farmers Market until her death three years ago.

J.T. shows off some of his seed catalogs and points out his favorite tomatoes: Celebrity, Big Beef, Early Girl, Brandywine, and Cherokee Purple. "You know, the only thing I like better than farming," he says with a smile, "is talking about it."

His grandfather was a rancher in Three Rivers, south of San Antonio, but his father was lured away to the oil fields because that work paid better. Like most country boys, J.T. joined Future Farmers and raised a few Holsteins on the twelve acres that his family owned. Cows were the reason he met Carolyn.

"She was a rodeo cowgirl," says J.T. "Her brother was showing cattle at the fair and so was I. That's where I met her."

He tried his hand at bull riding for a while, but that was just a "kid thing." In 1967, shortly after he and Carolyn were married, he was drafted and sent to Vietnam with the First Air Calvary Division. His tour lasted a year and three days. It's a time he's proud of, though the memories still haunt him.

When he came home, J.T. worked with his father and brother-in-law building houses, nearly fifty including his own, in and around Canton. In 1976, he decided to make a go at farming because he liked to see things grow.

"I still grow tomatoes the old-fashioned way, with bonemeal and cottonseed meal," he says as we ride around the farm in his Kubota with his dog Lucy, "and I cultivate with a tractor."

He drives past a line of peach trees that have just produced their final fruit of the season. For twenty-five days straight, the temperatures have been in the triple digits. "Even a few clouds would be a help. I've let the grass grow over some of my peppers to protect them," he says.

He's seen a lot of changes at the Dallas Farmers Market, but he rolls with the punches. Judy, one of his assistants, has just set him up on Facebook. She tells him that this will be a good way to stay in touch with customers. He's a little worried because he hasn't mastered turning on the computer. On his desk is a quote from John Wayne, one of his heroes: "Courage is being scared to death—but saddling up anyway."

PEACH PICO DE GALLO

*From Jill Lightner,
Edible Communities*

In midsummer, when local peaches are at their finest, it's nearly impossible to over-indulge. Of course, peach season coincides with the highest temperatures of the year, which makes it hard to get too excited about complicated cooking. Pico de gallo fits the bill—it's sweet and juicy but with plenty of kick from the addition of raw onion, garlic, and jalapeños. Served with fresh peach margaritas or daiquiris and tortilla chips, this simple snack is an ideal refreshment; if you find yourself in need an entire meal, we recommend it alongside Black Beer–Boiled Spiced Gulf Shrimp (page 125) or Grilled New York Strip Steak (page 115). Peach and Blackberry Cobbler (page 139) is the obvious dessert choice—because too much of a good thing is never enough.

1 LARGE PEACH, PEELED, PITTED, AND DICED
1 JALAPEÑO CHILE, SEEDED AND MINCED
¼ CUP DICED WHITE ONION
1 CLOVE GARLIC, MINCED

2 ROMA TOMATOES, DICED
JUICE OF 1 LIME
SALT
2 TSP CHOPPED FRESH CILANTRO

Serves 4

1 In a small bowl, gently combine the peach, jalapeño, onion, garlic, and tomatoes. Drizzle with the lime juice, season to taste with salt, and stir gently to blend. Taste and adjust the seasonings. Garnish with the cilantro.

PICKLED GREEN BEANS AND CARROTS
WITH BLISTERED TOMATOES

From Tim Byres, Smoke, Dallas

Chef Tim Byres keeps the wood fires stoked at his Smoke restaurant in Oak Cliff. Though southern-style barbecue and smoked meats are at the center of his menu, the restaurant also offers plenty of heritage-inspired vegetable dishes to satisfy the non–meat eater. In this recipe, a mélange of blistered tomatoes, pickled carrots with ginger, and green beans preserved in a fruity *guajillo* chile puree is warmed in a cast-iron skillet. For an added bit of color and flavor, serve it over a pool of Byres's Tomatillo Salsa Verde (page 11). Byres's résumé includes stints with Stephan Pyles, the Mansion on Turtle Creek, and the U.S. embassy in Brussels. He was recently named *Food & Wine* magazine's "The People's Best New Chef" for the Southwest region.

Edible Tip

Byres uses a channel knife to cut down the length of the carrots several times so that they have an interesting texture and appearance around the edge once they are sliced.

FOR THE PICKLED CARROTS:
1 LB CARROTS, PEELED AND CUT
  INTO ¼-INCH-THICK SLICES
1½ CUPS DISTILLED WHITE
  VINEGAR
2½ TBSP KOSHER SALT
6 TBSP SUGAR
1 MEDIUM PIECE FRESH GINGER,
  SLICED

FOR THE PICKLED GREEN BEANS:
2 DRIED GUAJILLO CHILES
2 CUPS DISTILLED WHITE VINEGAR

¼ CUP SHERRY VINEGAR
7 TBSP SUGAR
1 TBSP CHILI POWDER
2 TSP KOSHER SALT
1 DRIED BAY LEAF
1 LB GREEN BEANS, STEMMED

TO ASSEMBLE THE DISH:
1 TBSP OLIVE OIL
24–30 CHERRY TOMATOES

Serves 8

MAKE THE PICKLED CARROTS:

1 Combine the carrots, vinegar, salt, sugar, and ginger in a medium saucepan over medium-high heat. Bring the liquid to a boil; remove the saucepan from the heat. Allow the mixture to cool completely in the uncovered saucepan.

2 Transfer the carrots and pickling liquid to a bowl, cover, and refrigerate overnight or up to 1 week.

MAKE THE PICKLED GREEN BEANS:

3 Preheat the oven to 400°F. Place the dried chiles on a baking sheet. Place the baking sheet into the oven for 30 seconds to 1 minute to toast the chiles slightly. Remove and discard the stems and seeds.

4 Place the chiles in a small saucepan, and add enough water to just cover them. Bring to a simmer over medium heat. Remove from the heat and let the chiles sit for 15 minutes to rehydrate. Place the chiles and their liquid in a blender and process until smooth.

5 In a small saucepan, combine 1½ tablespoons of the guajillo paste with both vinegars and the sugar, chili powder, salt, and bay leaf. Bring to a boil over medium-high heat. Place the green beans in a bowl and pour the hot brine over the beans. Cover the beans and refrigerate overnight or up to 1 week.

6 Preheat a large cast-iron skillet over high heat. Once the pan is hot, add the olive oil and heat until it just begins to smoke.

7 Add the tomatoes to the hot skillet and shake them around until they are evenly blistered and heated through. Drain and add the pickled carrots and green beans, and sauté them quickly, merely to heat them through, but not to cook them any further.

TOMATILLO SALSA VERDE

From Tim Byres, Smoke, Dallas

The tomatillo verde, Spanish for "little green tomato," is not to be confused with its very distant relative, the tomato, whether red or green. Blame the Aztecs for the mix-up. They used the Nahuatl word *tomatl*, meaning "plump and round," for both. The shiny green fruit hidden under the tomatillo's papery sheath of leaves is mildly tart, and it is the tangy foundation for most Mexican green sauces.

Chef Tim Byres of Smoke in Dallas has devised a simple salsa recipe that can be served as a dip with tortilla chips or as a light, zesty condiment to spice up chicken, pork, or fish. For a vegetarian option, serve this recipe alongside his Pickled Green Beans and Carrots with Blistered Tomatoes (page 10).

1 LB FRESH TOMATILLOS, SKINS
  REMOVED, HALVED
½ YELLOW ONION, QUARTERED
2 JALAPEÑO CHILES, STEMMED AND
  SEEDED

5 CLOVES GARLIC, PEELED
½ CUP FRESH CILANTRO LEAVES
1 TSP KOSHER SALT

Serves 8

1 In a medium saucepan over medium heat, combine the tomatillos, onion, jalapeños, garlic, and 2 cups water. Bring to a simmer and cook for 10 minutes.

2 Using a slotted spoon, remove the tomatillos and vegetables from the cooking liquid to a medium bowl. Cool to room temperature. While they're cooling, return the saucepan to the heat and boil the cooking liquid until it is reduced to about ½ cup, about 6 minutes.

3 Pour the reduced cooking liquid into the bowl with the tomatillos. Place the bowl in the refrigerator and allow it to cool completely.

4 Place the chilled tomatillo mixture in a food processor or blender. Add the cilantro and salt. Blend until the salsa is completely smooth.

Edible Tips

◆ This salsa can be made in advance and kept covered in the refrigerator for 1 week.
◆ Add the cilantro *only* after the other ingredients have cooled, to retain color and flavor.

WATERMELON AND GOAT CHEESE STACKS

From Kelly Yandell,
TheMeaningofPie.com

There is nothing more emblematic of Texas summers than the sight of watermelons being sold out of the back of a pickup truck. Eaten straight off the rind or sprinkled with a little salt, watermelon is the embodiment of a southern summer. In this recipe, the country girl is dressed up a tad. Bite-size watermelon and goat cheese rounds are placed in red-and-white-striped stacks and topped with a bit of bacon, a fresh basil leaf, and a drizzle of balsamic vinegar. Perfect for a summer appetizer tray, it's visually playful and sublimely delicious. "When I pull herbs out of my garden, I love to taste them with whatever fruit or vegetables I have on hand," says food writer Kelly Yandell. "Sometimes, amazing things happen. This combination surprised me with its cinnamon flavor. The goat cheese mellows it out, and the bacon, well, I like that on just about everything."

1 SMALL SEEDLESS WATERMELON
   (WITH PLENTY LEFT OVER)
1 (8 OZ) LOG GOAT CHEESE, CHILLED
3 SLICES MEDIUM-THICK BACON,
   COOKED UNTIL CRISP

12 FRESH BASIL LEAVES
BALSAMIC VINEGAR FOR
   DRIZZLING

Makes 12 bite-size appetizers

1 Cut the watermelon into large disks, each about 1 inch thick. With a round cookie or biscuit cutter about 1½ inches in diameter, cut out 12 watermelon rounds, avoiding the seedy spots. Depending on the size of your watermelon, each large disk will yield 3 or 4 rounds. Set these onto paper towels briefly to drain the excess juice.

2 Cut the log of goat cheese into 12 disks of approximately the same thickness as the watermelon disks. Use the cookie cutter to trim the cheese to the same size as the watermelon. Cut each strip of bacon into 4 pieces.

3 To assemble the stack, start with a disk of watermelon. Top with a disk of goat cheese, a basil leaf, and finally, a piece of bacon. Just before serving, drizzle each bite with a little balsamic vinegar.

Edible Tips

• Seedless watermelons are not exactly seedless. Most contain small white seeds that are much easier to contend with or avoid than the big black ones. Look for spots without seeds when cutting out the disks. You can snack on the rest.
• If you are having trouble slicing your goat cheese, consider using a length of unflavored dental floss or fishing line. Hold the floss taut and press down through the cheese for a clean cut.

BLUEBERRY, PEACH, AND SWEET ONION SALAD

From Eva Greer, The Greer Farm, Daingerfield

Early summer harvest. Juicy peaches and sweet blueberries rest on leaves of spicy arugula with slivers of pickled onions strewn between them. Chef Eva Greer and her husband, Sid, say their farm has been in continuous operation since the mid-1840s. Prior to that, the land was home to the Caddo Indians. There are still old-style outbuildings and some that are made of hand-cut timbers. With its spring-fed lake and pick-your-own berry fields, Greer Farm evokes a simpler time.

Edible Tip

The remaining blueberry vinegar can be covered and stored in the refrigerator for up to 2 weeks.

8 RIPE PEACHES, PITTED AND HALVED
5 TBSP OLIVE OIL
2 CUPS FRESH BLUEBERRIES
¼ CUP SUGAR
1 CUP WHITE WINE VINEGAR
¾ CUP THINLY SLICED RED ONION, SALTED WITH KOSHER OR SEA SALT
4½ CUPS ARUGULA

Serves 6

1 Preheat the grill to medium-high. Brush the halved peaches with 1 tablespoon of the olive oil and grill skin side down until they begin to brown, about 3 minutes. Remove from the grill, let cool, and cut into ¼-inch-thick slices; set aside.

2 In a blender, combine 1 cup of the blueberries and the sugar and vinegar. Blend at medium speed until pureed. In a small bowl, whisk the remaining 4 tablespoons olive oil with 2 tablespoons of the blueberry vinegar. Rinse the salted onion slices and drain.

3 In a serving bowl, combine the arugula, onions, and grilled peaches and the remaining 1 cup blueberries. Drizzle with the vinaigrette to your liking and gently toss to combine. Serve immediately.

GULF FISH CEVICHE

From Jon Alexis,
TJ's Seafood Market, Dallas

Healthy and refreshing, ceviche is a great dish for a hot summer day. It's a beautiful assortment of local flavors: the mildness of fresh Gulf fish, the tartness of Texas citrus, and the spiciness of homegrown chiles. The acidity in the citrus juices pickles, or "cooks," the raw fish as it marinates. Every region of Central and South America has its preferred list of ingredients for ceviche. This recipe provides the basics, but every cook should create a version of his or her own. You can add grapefruit juice to your marinade, like they do in Chile. Serve in tostada shells or in a martini glass over greens. Put a scoop on a cucumber wheel and garnish with red bell pepper and cayenne. Don't think of this as a recipe: think of it as a blank culinary canvas. Your creation is limited only by your imagination and what's in season.

Edible Tips

Gulf shrimp or scallops may be added. Boil these for 1–2 minutes before marinating. For sweeter ceviche, add ¾ cup chopped mango, pineapple, or papaya right before serving. For a creamier ceviche, add ¼ cup mayonnaise or sour cream. For a cooler ceviche, add ½ cup diced peeled cucumber or celery. For a spicier ceviche, add a dash or two more of Tabasco or sriracha sauce.

2 LB FRESH TEXAS GULF FISH FILLETS (ANY COMBINATION OF SNAPPER, RED FISH, TILEFISH, MAHI-MAHI, OR SPECKLED SEA TROUT), CUT INTO ½-INCH CUBES
DASH OF TABASCO SAUCE
2 TSP SALT
1 CUP SEEDED AND COARSELY CHOPPED RIPE LOCAL TOMATOES
1 SERRANO CHILE, SEEDED AND FINELY DICED
½ MEDIUM RED ONION, FINELY DICED
½ TSP DRIED OREGANO OR 1½ TSP CHOPPED FRESH OREGANO
½ CUP FRESH LEMON JUICE
½ CUP FRESH LIME JUICE
2 TBSP CHOPPED FRESH CILANTRO
1 AVOCADO, PEELED, PITTED, AND CUT INTO ¾-INCH WEDGES (OPTIONAL)
2 LIMES, SLICED (OPTIONAL)
TORTILLA CHIPS

Serves 6–8

1 In a large glass casserole dish, toss together the fish, Tabasco, salt, tomatoes, chile, onion, and oregano.

2 Pour in the lemon and lime juices, thoroughly drenching and combining all the ingredients. Cover and place in the refrigerator. After 1 hour, stir well; then return to the refrigerator for 4–5 more hours.

3 Before serving, stir in the cilantro. Garnish the plates with avocado wedges and lime slices and serve with tortilla chips.

CHILLED WATERMELON SOUP

From Beverly Thomas, Cold Springs Farm, Weatherford

When Beverly Thomas was growing up in rural Mississippi, midsummer Wednesdays were special. "My grandparents operated a general store," says Thomas, "and on Wednesdays, Granny and I would head to the Jackson Farmers Market to pick up watermelons." Thomas's grandmother taught her the nuances of thumping and weighing and, of course, all about the stem. According to Granny, truly fresh watermelons have a very green stem all the way to the end. "Granny was a very discerning customer. We would load up the back of the truck, but not until after she'd haggled with the farmer. She never paid more than a nickel per watermelon." By the time they arrived home, a watermelon-hungry mob would be waiting at the store. "Granny would sell all the watermelons in about twenty minutes, but she always saved a couple for Pawpaw and me. We'd devour them that afternoon; then we'd have to wait until the next Wednesday for more."

1 SMALL JALAPEÑO CHILE, SEEDED, DEVEINED, AND FINELY CHOPPED
2 TBSP CHOPPED FRESH LEMON BASIL
1 TBSP EXTRA-VIRGIN LIGHT OLIVE OIL
1 TBSP BALSAMIC VINEGAR
3 CUPS DICED SEEDED WATERMELON
1 SEEDLESS CUCUMBER, PEELED AND CUBED
1 CUP FRESH ORANGE JUICE
1 CUP FRESH PINEAPPLE JUICE
½ CUP BUTTERMILK
3 TBSP FRESH LIME JUICE
SALT
FRESHLY GROUND BLACK PEPPER

FOR THE GARNISH:
6 OZ FRESH FETA CHEESE, CRUMBLED
FRESH MINT LEAVES

Serves 6

1 Place the jalapeño, lemon basil, olive oil, and vinegar in a food processor and pulse until blended. Add the watermelon and cucumber in small batches and process until smooth.

2 Slowly pour in the orange juice, pineapple juice, buttermilk, and lime juice and pulse until the liquids are well incorporated into the mixture. Add salt and pepper to taste. Chill, covered, at least 8 hours, or overnight.

3 When ready to serve, pour into individual bowls and garnish with a sprinkle of feta and fresh mint.

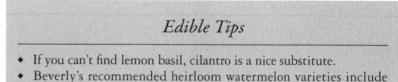

Edible Tips

- If you can't find lemon basil, cilantro is a nice substitute.
- Beverly's recommended heirloom watermelon varieties include Ali Baba, Orangeglo, and Osh Kirgizia.

CHILLED BEET SOUP

From Kelly Yandell,
TheMeaningofPie.com

Gorgeous stacks of ruby red beets are a dramatic sight at local farmers' markets during the cool weather months. On a pleasant spring morning, Kelly Yandell, the home cook behind the comfort-food blog *The Meaning of Pie*, devised this soup recipe while on a stroll through the Dallas Farmers Market. "Photography has made me very aware of the beauty of vegetables and fruits in their natural state," says Yandell. "I wanted to create something that lets the beets show off their impressive color and unique flavor." In this soup, the earthy beets are brightened by a touch of lemon and subtly sweetened with local honey. Depending on your preference, serve either slightly warmed or chilled.

Edible Tips

♦ Beets can easily stain your hands and clothes, so work carefully. Stains on your hands can be removed by scrubbing them with salt or lemon juice and water.

♦ Save the greens from the beets. They're flavorful and highly nutritious and can be prepared in much the same way as other sturdy greens.

5 MEDIUM BEETS, PEELED AND CUT INTO ¾-INCH CHUNKS
6 CARROTS, PEELED AND CUT INTO ¾-INCH CHUNKS
1 TBSP GRATED LEMON ZEST
2 TBSP FRESH LEMON JUICE
2 TSP FRESH MINCED ROSEMARY
¼ CUP LOCAL HONEY
½ TSP KOSHER SALT

Serves 6

1 Place the beets and carrots in a large pot and cover generously with water; bring the water to a boil. Allow the vegetables to cook over medium-high heat until they are fork-tender, about 15 minutes.

2 Remove the pot from the heat and measure out 3 cups of the cooking water; reserve. Drain the beets and carrots in a colander. Return the beets, carrots, and reserved cooking water to the pot.

3 Using an immersion blender (or working in several batches in a regular blender), puree the mixture until smooth. Stir in the lemon zest and juice, rosemary, honey, and salt until well combined.

4 You can let the soup cool and serve slightly warm, or cover and refrigerate to serve chilled.

CHORIZO-STUFFED DATES

*From Blaine Staniford,
Grace, Fort Worth*

One bite of these caramel-flavored, meat-stuffed, spicy little poppers and you'll be hooked. They have layers of taste, with four types of ground chiles and a wrap of applewood-smoked bacon. Rich, sticky, and addictive, dates are one of the oldest cultivated foods on earth. Researchers have uncovered fossils showing date-growing palm trees from more than fifty million years ago. Dates may be Middle Eastern in origin, but the seasonings here say Texas. Executive chef Blaine Staniford of Grace in downtown Fort Worth is one of the culinary world's rising stars, and this recipe will show you why.

2 TBSP PEANUT OIL
½ LB GROUND BEEF
½ LB GROUND PORK
1 CLOVE GARLIC, MINCED
½ MEDIUM YELLOW ONION, MINCED
3 DRIED CHIPOTLE CHILES, GROUND
2 ROASTED ANCHO CHILES, GROUND
1 ROASTED GUAJILLO CHILE, GROUND
1 ROASTED DE ARBOL CHILE, GROUND
SALT
FRESHLY GROUND BLACK PEPPER
1 LB MEDJOOL DATES (ABOUT 25)
13 SLICES APPLEWOOD-SMOKED BACON
25 TOOTHPICKS

Serves 6

1 Preheat the oven to 350°F. Line a baking sheet with parchment paper.

2 Heat a medium sauté pan over medium heat. Add the peanut oil and heat until it shimmers. Add both ground meats and cook, breaking up any clumps, until they begin to brown, about 5 minutes.

3 Add the garlic, onion, and ground chiles. Season with salt and pepper to taste. Remove from the heat and allow to cool to the point where you can touch the mixture without getting burned.

4 While the chorizo is cooling, cut the dates open lengthwise and remove the pits. Gently stuff about 1 tablespoon of the seasoned meat into each of them.

5 Cut the slices of bacon in half crosswise. Wrap each date with one short piece of bacon and secure with a toothpick.

6 Place the dates on the prepared baking sheet and bake until the bacon is slightly crisp, 10–12 minutes. Serve warm.

DILL AND CAPER GULF SHRIMP DIP

From Jon Alexis,
TJ's Seafood Market, Dallas

Each summer in Texas coastal towns from Port Arthur to Port Isabel, the commercial shrimp season begins with the Blessing of the Fleet. At festivities, clergy and well-wishers bid safe passage and a bountiful catch to shrimpers as they set out in their trawlers for open water. According to seafood purveyor Jon Alexis, brown shrimp from the Gulf of Mexico are prized for their size, flavor, and texture. Habitat determines how shrimp taste, and because brown shrimp feed on iodine-rich kelp, their meat has a bolder, heartier flavor. Though most chefs consider wild Gulf shrimp to be among the finest in the world, it is estimated that nearly 90 percent of the shrimp consumed in the United States comes from foreign sources. Not all shrimp are created equal. For the tastiest, healthiest shrimp and fish, ask your fishmonger and restaurant owner for the local catch.

¾ LB (16–20 COUNT) GULF SHRIMP, PEELED AND DEVEINED
2 TSP SALT
1 (8 OZ) PACKAGE CREAM CHEESE
½ CUP MAYONNAISE
1 TBSP FINELY DICED RED BELL PEPPER
1½ TSP CHOPPED FRESH PARSLEY
1½ TSP CHOPPED FRESH DILL
1½ TSP FINELY DICED RED ONION
1½ TSP CHOPPED CAPERS
1½ TSP FINELY DICED SHALLOTS
1½ TSP CAJUN BLACKENING POWDER
¼ TSP WORCESTERSHIRE SAUCE
CRACKERS, TOAST POINTS, PITA CHIPS, OR CRUDITÉS FOR SERVING

Serves 8

1 Bring 8 cups of water to a rapid boil in a medium saucepan, add the shrimp and salt, and cook until the shrimp is done, about 6 minutes. The shrimp will have an opaque center when fully cooked. Drain, and then set under cold running water until the shrimp are cool enough to handle. Slice the shrimp into medium chunks; set aside.

2 In a medium bowl, whip the cream cheese and mayonnaise together with an electric mixer until smooth. Stir in the bell pepper, parsley, dill, red onion, capers, shallots, blackening powder, and Worcestershire sauce until well blended.

3 Fold in the shrimp and chill before serving. Serve with crackers, toast points, pita chips, or freshly cut crudités.

TOMATO AND MOZZARELLA SALAD
WITH WALNUT-BASIL PESTO

*From John Stout, Celebration
Restaurant, Dallas*

The folks at Celebration Restaurant are committed to local farmers, so much so that they sponsor a farmers' market in the restaurant parking lot every Saturday during the growing season. "These are the true farmers," says chef John Stout. "They really care about the small restaurant guys like us. I cannot say enough about the quality and the freshness of their produce." At Celebration's Saturday market, neighbors drop by to purchase produce, meats, and artisanal food products as well as local art. Stout sources from J.T. Lemley, Stacy Saxon of Saxon Farms, and Virginia and Winford Sides of Sides Pea Farm, among others. For this salad, he pairs slices of Mr. Lemley's delicious tomatoes with smooth rounds of Mozzarella Company's mozzarella and tops each stack with a spoonful of walnut-basil pesto.

Edible Tip

After dressing the salad, you can refrigerate any leftover pesto for up to 1 week.

FOR THE PESTO:
1 CUP UNSALTED, RAW WALNUT
  MEATS
1 TSP CHOPPED GARLIC
2 GREEN ONIONS (WHITE AND
  LIGHT GREEN PARTS ONLY),
  CHOPPED
1 CUP OLIVE OIL
1 CUP FRESHLY GRATED PARMESAN
  CHEESE
1 CUP PACKED FRESH BASIL LEAVES
¼ CUP PACKED FRESH PARSLEY

½ TSP SALT
½ TSP FINELY GROUND BLACK
  PEPPER

FOR THE SALAD:
4 LARGE TOMATOES, SLICED ¼ INCH
  THICK (YOU'LL NEED 16 SLICES)
16 OZ MOZZARELLA CHEESE, SLICED
  ¼ INCH THICK (YOU'LL NEED
  8 SLICES)

Serves 8

MAKE THE PESTO:

1 Place the walnuts, garlic, and green onions in a food processor with approximately 1 tablespoon of the olive oil. Pulse several times until the garlic and walnuts are coarsely chopped.

2 Add the Parmesan, basil, parsley, salt, and pepper. As you pulse the ingredients, add ¼ cup of the olive oil down the feeder tube in a thin stream to create an emulsion. You may add it slightly more quickly after that, until the entire cup has been incorporated. Set aside. (After dressing the salad, any leftover pesto can be refrigerated for up to 1 week.)

ASSEMBLE THE SALAD:

3 Pile 2 slices of tomato on each of 8 serving plates. Lay a slice of mozzarella on each stack. Pour a generous spoonful of pesto over the mozzarella. Serve immediately.

HEIRLOOM TOMATO SALAD WITH BLACKBERRY MOLASSES VINAIGRETTE

From Eric Hunter, Fire Oak Grill, Weatherford

The Fire Oak Grill on Weatherford's historic downtown square has a menu full of quintessential Texas specialties like saucy braised brisket and Dr Pepper–marinated pork. But chef Eric Hunter also prepares incredibly fresh and creative sides and salads, thanks to his neighbor Beverly Thomas, who grows an innovative variety of rare and heirloom vegetables and fruits at her Cold Springs Farm. Hunter, a native of Fort Worth, served as chef de cuisine at the Lonesome Dove Western Bistro in his hometown and has also appeared with chef Tim Love on the Food Network's *Iron Chef*. Wearing cowboy hats with their chefs' coats, Team Love outgunned Iron Chef Masaharu Morimoto. This salad tosses together Cold Springs microgreens, cucumber, fennel, and baby heirloom tomatoes with a sweet vinaigrette of Texas blackberries, shallots, and molasses.

Edible Tip

The remaining half cup of vinaigrette will last for 3 days in the refrigerator.

FOR THE VINAIGRETTE:

1 TSP CANOLA OR GRAPESEED OIL
1 SHALLOT, MINCED
1 PINT FRESH BLACKBERRIES, RINSED
⅓ CUP RED WINE VINEGAR
⅓ CUP MOLASSES
½ CUP WHITE WINE VINEGAR
½ CUP EXTRA-VIRGIN OLIVE OIL
SALT
FRESHLY GROUND BLACK PEPPER

FOR THE SALAD:

2 BULBS BABY FENNEL, FRONDS REMOVED

½ ENGLISH CUCUMBER
1 PINT MIXED HEIRLOOM CHERRY OR GRAPE TOMATOES, HALVED
1 TSP FINELY CHOPPED FRESH THYME
¼ CUP WHITE BALSAMIC VINEGAR
SALT
FRESHLY GROUND BLACK PEPPER
¼ CUP CRUMBLED GOAT CHEESE
¼ CUP MICROGREENS, PREFERABLY ARUGULA, BULL'S BLOOD, AND TATSOI

Serves 6–8

MAKE THE VINAIGRETTE:

1 In a small saucepan over high heat, warm the oil until it shimmers. Add the shallot and sauté until translucent, about 6 minutes. Add the blackberries and gently shake the pan until the berries start to cook (you'll see their juices spreading across the bottom of the pan). Lower the heat to medium, add the red wine vinegar and molasses, and simmer for 5 minutes.

2 Using an immersion blender, puree the mixture until completely smooth. Push the puree through a fine-mesh strainer into a bowl. Place the puree in a blender, add the white wine vinegar at a low speed until completely blended, then slowly add the olive oil, blending until the mixture thickens. Season to taste with salt and pepper.

MAKE THE SALAD:

3 Shave the fennel into thin slices using a mandoline if you have one. Cut the cucumber half in half lengthwise, and then place the pieces flat side down and once again cut each piece in half lengthwise. Then cut the cucumber quarters crosswise into thin slices.

4 In a large bowl, gently toss the cucumber, fennel, and tomatoes with the thyme and balsamic vinegar. Season with salt and pepper to taste.

5 Divide the mixture among the salad plates and crumble the goat cheese over the salads. Scatter the microgreens on top of the cheese. Drizzle a small amount of the blackberry vinaigrette on top and around the plates (about ¼ cup total).

STARTERS

23

MEDITERRANEAN SALAD WITH LEMON DRESSING

From Vickie Smolek, Grapevine Grains, Grapevine

A lot of fruits and vegetables that grow in the Mediterranean region flourish in Texas. During the summer, farmers' markets and home gardens from Tyler to Marfa teem with ripe tomatoes, cucumbers, and fresh herbs. Vickie Smolek, who sells her non-GMO granola and grains at area farmers' markets, turns to this light summer salad in the hot months. "The basil is fresh, and everything is growing," she says. "I make it a lot." She was inspired by a salad she enjoyed in Morocco; the combination of cucumber and tomato is ubiquitous in Mediterranean countries.

2 LARGE CUCUMBERS, DICED (PEELING AND SEEDING ARE OPTIONAL)
4 RIPE MEDIUM TOMATOES, DICED
2 SMALL RED ONIONS, DICED
4–6 CLOVES GARLIC, CRUSHED AND CHOPPED

6 TBSP FRESH LEMON JUICE
2 TSP CHOPPED FRESH BASIL
SEA SALT
FRESHLY GROUND BLACK PEPPER
3 TBSP EXTRA-VIRGIN OLIVE OIL

Serves 4

1 Combine the cucumbers, tomatoes, onions, and garlic in a medium bowl.

2 In a small bowl, whisk together the lemon juice, basil, and salt and pepper to taste. Slowly drizzle in the olive oil as you continue whisking. Pour the dressing over the vegetables and toss gently to coat. Serve chilled.

PORTOBELLO AND GOAT CHEESE MEATLESS MEATBALLS

From Jim Severson, Sevy's Grill, Dallas

Whether you're serving them as appetizers or over pasta as a vegetarian entrée, these mushroom and goat cheese "meatballs" are guaranteed to be a savory hit. Firm-textured portobellos are rolled together with chives, tangy goat cheese from Paula Lambert's Mozzarella Company, spices, and panko breadcrumbs. Chef Jim "Sevy" Severson is well-known for his creative American cuisine, but he is also revered for his generous spirit. Since his days as chef at Dakota's in downtown Dallas, he has been a supporter of the Dallas Farmers Market, recruiting chefs for its popular weekend cooking classes. In honor of his good deeds and hard work, there's a scholarship fund for culinary arts students at El Centro College named for him.

1 LB PORTOBELLO MUSHROOMS
(3–4 MEDIUM/LARGE)
2 TSP OLIVE OIL
2 TBSP PLUS 1 TSP MINCED GARLIC
1 TSP SALT
½ TSP SEASONED SALT
⅛ TSP GARLIC SALT
⅛ TSP ONION SALT
⅛ TSP FRESHLY GROUND BLACK PEPPER
⅛ TSP CAYENNE

1 TSP MINCED SHALLOTS
1 TBSP MINCED FRESH CHIVES
¼ CUP PANKO BREADCRUMBS
2 OZ GOAT CHEESE, AT ROOM TEMPERATURE
½ CUP FRESHLY GRATED PARMESAN CHEESE
1 TBSP MINCED FRESH BASIL
1 EGG WHITE

Serves 16 as an appetizer

1 Preheat oven to 325 degrees F. Trim the stems of the mushrooms to about ½ inch long. Place the mushrooms topside down on a baking sheet and sprinkle with the olive oil, garlic, and salt. Bake until the mushrooms are cooked through and the garlic is browned, about 15 minutes. Cool to room temperature.

2 Pulse the mushrooms in a food processor until coarsely chopped. Transfer to a large bowl and add the seasoned salt, garlic salt, onion salt, pepper, cayenne, shallots, chives, and breadcrumbs. Toss with clean hands to mix. Blend in the goat cheese, Parmesan, and basil, then pour on the egg white and mix thoroughly. Cover and chill in the refrigerator for 30 minutes, allowing the crumbs to absorb the moisture.

3 Preheat the oven to 375°F. Line a baking sheet with parchment paper.

4 Roll the mixture into golf ball–size balls, place on the prepared baking sheet, and bake until they begin to brown, 10–15 minutes. Serve hot.

SHIITAKE MUSHROOM AND CHÈVRE STRUDEL

From Brian C. Luscher,
The Grape, Dallas

Chef Brian Luscher's savory mushroom and goat cheese strudel can be cut into appetizer-size portions or served with a hearty soup for lunch. Fresh organic mushrooms are sautéed with shallots and onions and mixed with crumbles of creamy chèvre, then rolled in a light puff pastry. At Texas Organic Mushrooms in Denison, Elizabeth McCarthy and her late husband Joseph began growing their organic shiitake mushrooms in 1990 on their family farm. Their first customer was chef Dean Fearing, who was then at the Mansion on Turtle Creek. Today, more than twenty years later, he still buys Texas certified organic shiitakes for Fearing's in the Ritz-Carlton, as do chef Brian Luscher and many others.

¼ CUP OLIVE OIL
3 SHALLOTS, MINCED
1 DRIED BAY LEAF
2 LB ORGANIC TEXAS SHIITAKE
   MUSHROOMS, CHOPPED
½ CUP SHERRY
2 TBSP UNSALTED BUTTER
2–3 CLOVES GARLIC, MINCED
½ TSP SALT
1 TBSP FRESHLY GROUND BLACK
   PEPPER

2 TBSP CHOPPED FRESH THYME
2 TBSP THINLY SLICED FRESH
   CHIVES
8 OZ GOAT CHEESE, CRUMBLED
1 SHEET FROZEN PUFF PASTRY,
   THAWED
1 EGG, BEATEN WITH 1 TSP WATER

Serves 8 as an appetizer

1 Warm the olive oil in a medium sauté pan over medium heat. Add the shallots and bay leaf. Cook, stirring a few times, until the shallots are translucent but not browned. Add the mushrooms and cook, stirring, until they brown, about 2 minutes.

2 Cover the pan and let the mushrooms cook in their own juices until they start to soften, about 5 minutes. Add the sherry all at once and scrape up any browned bits from the bottom of the pan. Add the butter and garlic and cook, stirring, for 1 minute. Add the salt, pepper, thyme, and chives. Remove the bay leaf.

3 Pour the mixture onto a rimmed baking sheet and place, uncovered, in the refrigerator to cool completely; then transfer to a bowl and mix with the goat cheese.

4 Preheat the oven to 425°F. Lightly grease a baking sheet.

5 Place the puff pastry sheet on a lightly floured work surface. Place the filling off-center lengthwise down the pastry. With a pastry brush, brush the egg wash around the perimeter of the dough. Fold the long edges into the center, overlapping them over the filling. Flip the strudel so the seam is on the bottom and seal the short ends by folding them under or pinching.

6 Place on the prepared baking sheet. Bake until golden brown, about 20 minutes. Let cool for at least 5 minutes before slicing.

FRIED SQUASH BLOSSOMS WITH HERBED GOAT CHEESE

*From Matt Reddick, Il Cane Rosso,
Dallas*

Bouquets of soft yellow- and orange-hued squash blossoms are a vision at farmers' markets. These lovelies are fragile and perishable and will never be your typical grocery store fare. As an appetizer, stuffed with herbed goat cheese and lightly battered, squash blossoms are divine. Il Cane Rosso, in the heart of Deep Ellum, not only makes the best Neapolitan pizza in Dallas, but also offers a creative menu of mouthwatering appetizers. Chef Matt Reddick makes this dish with basil and squash blossoms from Tassione Farms in Stephenville and chèvre from his Deep Ellum neighbor Paula Lambert at the Mozzarella Company.

Edible Tips

• Make sure your squash blossoms are fresh. Open them up and check for any bugs. Cucumber beetles and drowsy bees love these things.
• Rice flour, found at most Asian markets, makes a coating that's crispier than regular flour and holds together longer. If rice flour is unavailable, use a mixture of half cornstarch and half all-purpose flour.

FOR THE HERBED GOAT CHEESE:
1½ CUPS ROOM-TEMPERATURE
   GOAT CHEESE
1 TBSP CHOPPED FRESH BASIL
1 TBSP CHOPPED FRESH OREGANO
1 TSP CHOPPED FRESH ROSEMARY
½ TSP SALT
½ TSP FRESHLY GROUND BLACK
   PEPPER

FOR THE BATTER:
1 CUP RICE FLOUR

TO FRY THE SQUASH BLOSSOMS:
12 SQUASH BLOSSOMS
CANOLA OIL FOR FRYING

Serves 6

1 In a small bowl, mix together the goat cheese, basil, oregano, rosemary, salt, and pepper until well blended.

2 In a medium bowl, whisk 1¼ cups cold water into the rice flour until well blended.

3 Remove the stems from the squash blossoms and give the flowers a gentle rinse; they are rather fragile. Stuff the blossoms with about 2 tablespoons of the herbed goat cheese. Don't overfill them; they should not be bulging. Gently give the tops of each blossom a twist to seal in the cheese.

4 Heat the oil to 350°F in an electric deep fryer or Dutch oven. If using a Dutch oven, set the pot over medium-high heat and use a candy thermometer to track the temperature of the oil.

5 Once the oil is hot, dip the blossoms, one at a time, into the batter, until fully covered. Use tongs to carefully place the battered blossoms into the hot oil, and fry in 2 batches until golden brown. Remove them to a plate lined with paper towels. Serve immediately, while still hot.

CHAPTER 2

SOUPS, SANDWICHES, AND SUCH

Though the heading sounds tame, there's a Texas twist to each of these recipes. We love these quirky little master-pieces—more Picasso than Rembrandt—not beholden to any formal meal or to a set time of the day. We insist that you mix it up. Why not Wild Boar Pozole for breakfast or Smoked Cheddar Biscuits at midnight? Let loose with a fried green tomato or a One-Ball Squash Sandwich. Nosh on an afternoon batch of Cheesy Blonde Bread or a Swine Blue Taco. Get crazy with it. These are the recipes for those days when the schedule's gone out the window, your cravings are strange, and there are no rules.

TOMATO AND CHEDDAR FLATBREAD WITH RUNNY EGG

*From Robert Lyford, Patina Green
Home and Market, McKinney*

What does a chef prepare for himself after a day of cooking for others? This is the go-to dish for chef Robert Lyford of Patina Green Home and Market. "Breakfast, lunch, or dinner, I have an obsession for runny eggs," says Lyford. "Not just any egg, but a pasture-raised Turning Ranch egg from Ladonia. I've yet to find a better-tasting egg yolk. The yolk is the star of this dish!" He pairs it with a ripe local tomato, nine-month aged cheddar cheese from Veldhuizen Family Farm in Dublin, Texas, and a crispy flatbread. Patina Green is located on the square in historic McKinney. The store sells antiques and decorative home items as well as local produce, dairy products, and artisan foods which chef Lyford features in his ever-changing lunch menu.

Edible Tip

Naan is a popular Indian flatbread. It can be found at many grocery stores and most Middle Eastern markets. Pita bread can be substituted if naan is not available.

1 (8 OZ) PIECE CHEDDAR CHEESE
4 PIECES NAAN, ABOUT 4 X 6 INCHES EACH
1 RIPE LARGE TOMATO OR 2 ROMA TOMATOES, CUT INTO ¼-INCH-THICK SLICES
4 TBSP OLIVE OIL
4 PASTURE-RAISED EGGS
SEA SALT
FRESHLY GROUND BLACK PEPPER

Serves 4

1 Line the bottom of the oven with foil for easy cleanup and preheat to 450°F.

2 Using a vegetable peeler, shave the cheese in long strips evenly over the naan. Arrange the tomato slices on top on each piece of naan, spacing the slices out evenly over the shaved cheese, and then drizzle each with 1 tablespoon olive oil. Crack one egg onto the center of each piece of flatbread. Try to rest the egg in between the tomatoes, so that it doesn't slide around.

3 Season the flatbreads with sea salt and pepper to taste and place directly on the center oven rack. Bake until the naan is crispy and the egg is set to your liking, 7–10 minutes. Serve immediately.

ONE-BALL SQUASH SANDWICH

*From Robert Lyford, Patina Green
Home and Market, McKinney*

One-Ball squash is a little summer squash—round, yellow, and reminiscent of a billiard ball, hence the name. Chef Robert Lyford is an advocate for local farmers and has long believed in being creative with what nature delivers. "Most of the crops were dying on the vine from the Texas heat," says Lyford. "All I had to work with was One-Ball squash, and we had lots of it, all from Mr. Lemley's farm in Canton." He drizzled the squash with some Texas Olive Ranch olive oil, roasted it, and laid it out on Empire Baking Company's savory sourdough. Next came a handful of arugula, a slice of a sweet Texas 1015 onion, and a creamy layer of chèvre. The rest was history. It quickly became one of Patina Green's signature sandwiches. It's equally delicious served as is or as a grilled panini sandwich.

Edible Tips

- Yellow crookneck squash can be substituted for the One-Ball squash.
- Any sweet onion can replace the Texas 1015 onion.
- A nonstick pan may be substituted for the panini press. Take care to keep the sandwiches' filling inside the bread when turning them over.

1 TEXAS 1015 SWEET ONION (SEE EDIBLE TIPS BELOW)
6 TBSP EXTRA-VIRGIN OLIVE OIL
3 TSP SEA SALT
2 ONE-BALL SQUASH (SEE EDIBLE TIPS BELOW)
6 SLICES SOURDOUGH BREAD
4 OZ GOAT CHEESE
2 OZ ARUGULA, CHOPPED

Makes 3 sandwiches

1 Preheat the oven to 425°F. Line 2 baking sheets with parchment paper.

2 Slice the onion into ⅛-inch-thick rounds. In a large bowl, gently toss the onion slices with 3 tablespoons of the olive oil and 2 teaspoons of the salt. Spread in a single layer on one of the prepared baking sheets and roast until lightly caramelized, 10–15 minutes.

3 While the onions are cooking, slice the squash into ½-inch-thick rounds and toss with the remaining 3 tablespoons olive oil and 1 teaspoon salt. Spread in a single layer on the other prepared baking sheet. Bake until the slices are lightly browned, 7–10 minutes.

4 To assemble the sandwiches, lay out the bread and spread a layer of goat cheese on each slice. On 3 slices of bread, lay out a layer of roasted squash slices and top the squash with roasted onions and chopped arugula. Top with the remaining 3 slices of bread.

5 If desired, grill the sandwiches on a nonstick panini press on medium-high heat until the bread is golden brown on both sides. Cool on a rack for 2 minutes, and then slice on the diagonal and indulge.

GRANDMARY'S FRIED GREEN TOMATOES

From Karen Jacobs, Coppell Farmers Market steering committee member

GrandMary was a term of endearment for Karen Jacobs's mother. It was the name used by her first grandchild, and it stuck. When Jacobs and her husband lived near her parents in Thomasville, Georgia, GrandMary introduced Jacobs to fried green tomatoes. "My mom passed away in 1989, so I am now the Queen of Fried Green Tomatoes," says Jacobs, "and this is our recipe." Green tomatoes used to be scarce in North Texas. Now, knowing farmers and even grocers make sure to have some in season. Tart and crunchy, fried green tomatoes are delicious on their own. But Oddfellows, a Dallas restaurant, turns them into a fried-green-tomato BLT, piling bacon, lettuce, and avocado onto ciabatta smeared with a little mayo.

Edible Tip

This recipe calls for hard green tomatoes, not pink ones. (No cheating.)

2 EGGS
½ CUP WHOLE MILK
1 CUP SELF-RISING FLOUR
1 TSP SALT, PLUS MORE TO TASTE
1 TSP FRESHLY GROUND BLACK PEPPER, PLUS MORE TO TASTE

CANOLA OR GRAPESEED OIL FOR FRYING
4 HARD GREEN TOMATOES, SLICED INTO ROUNDS ABOUT ¼ INCH THICK

Serves 4

1 Mix the eggs and milk together in a small bowl. Combine the flour, salt, and pepper in a pie plate.

2 Pour oil to a depth of ½ inch in a deep pot. Over medium-high heat, warm the oil to 350°F, using a candy thermometer to check the temperature. Dunk each tomato slice first in the egg mixture, then cover each side in the flour mixture. Gently lay the tomato slices in the hot oil, being careful not to crowd them.

3 When the slices are golden brown on the bottom, in 2–3 minutes, flip them over with tongs, being careful not to splash the oil. Turn each slice only once, or the coating will crumble off. When the tomatoes are golden brown on both sides, drain them on a paper towel–lined plate. Season to taste with salt and pepper while they're hot.

FRIED-GREEN-TOMATO BLT

MATT AND HEATHER HAMILTON

The Local Yocal Farm to Market, McKinney

In a small town thirty miles from Dallas, there's a vibrant local food scene that's the envy of its big-city neighbors. The food boom in historic downtown McKinney has been fostered by a well-managed farmers' market, a talented group of chefs, and an ambitious young rancher whose marketing efforts helped tie the pieces together.

Rancher Matt Hamilton and his wife, Heather, became the hub of the wheel when they decided to open a butcher shop just off McKinney's newly revitalized central square. Matt's family had been ranching since 1905, but it was 2008 when he and his father decided to convert to grass-fed practices.

"Finally we had this great product, but we couldn't find a quality meat processor," says Hamilton. "We wanted to give our customers fresh meat, not frozen."

Frustrated with their options, they bought a building on a downtown side street in 2010 and opened their Local Yocal Farm to Market. They began custom cutting not only their own meat but the meats of other cottage producers as well. And they didn't stop there. They added display shelves and coolers and filled them with an assortment of local eggs, dairy products, produce, and breads, a one-stop shop for locavores that has continued to grow.

In a serendipitous stroke of timing, only a block away chef Craig Brundege (Spago Beverly Hills), sous-chef Ngoc Ngo (Abacus and Five Sixty), and co-owner Brandon Horrocks (Culinary Institute of America) were preparing to open their gourmet hamburger restaurant, Square Burger. They needed grass-fed beef and lots of it. It was a

rancher's dream. Local Yocal was exactly what they were looking for. Within six weeks of their opening, Square Burger was declared one of Dallas–Fort Worth's finest by *Dallas Morning News* critic Leslie Brenner, who made special note of the custom ground beef.

Meanwhile, on the other side of the square, chef Robert Lyford (Mansion on Turtle Creek and Ciudad) was opening an epicurean lunch counter and antiques store called Patina Green Home and Market with his wife, Kaci, and mother-in-law, Luann Van Winckel. Local Yocal's fresh meats quickly found their way onto Patina Green's menu. On his popular cheddar cheese biscuit, Lyford uses Local Yocal's smoked ham and his neighbor Leslie Luscombe's award-winning jalapeño jelly.

Lyford notes, "The best part of downtown McKinney is the community of small businesses. We aren't only concerned with our own business. We all support the success of each other. Our town is one of the last gems in the metroplex and we have one of the greatest farmers' markets in the country."

Organic grower and McKinney local Tom Motley also applauds McKinney's farmers' market for creating a savvy consumer and paving the way for this local food renaissance. "Cindy Johnson, the director of McKinney Farmers Market, deserves the biggest organic bouquet from all of us gardeners, chefs, foodies, and merchants on the square," says Motley. "The farmers' market has always been a venue for educating customers on organic, sustainable farming practices. This was a natural progression."

BEER-BRAISED AND GRILLED BRATS WITH ONIONS AND JUNIPER

From Elissa Altman, Edible Communities, Inc.

This nod to the large population of German immigrants who settled chunks of the great state elevates mild sausage from good (who doesn't love a good sausage?) to delirium-inducing greatness. Perfect for backyard barbecues, tailgates, and cool autumn dinners the night before the big game, brats are simmered in dark beer with a handful of earthy spices and red onion, then grilled to a crackling snap. Served on warm buns of your choice, they'll have you shouting *"How 'bout them Cowboys!"* in no time.

Edible Tip

You can find juniper berries at Kurry King (go to www. DallasSpiceMarket.com).

6 (12 OZ) BOTTLES DARK BEER
6 LARGE RED ONIONS, THINLY
   SLICED INTO ROUNDS
1 TBSP JUNIPER BERRIES
1 TBSP CARAWAY SEEDS
1 TBSP BLACK PEPPERCORNS

2 LB BRATWURST
FRANKFURTER BUNS
SPICY MUSTARD

Serves 6

1 Bring the beer to a low boil in a large stockpot over medium-high heat. Add the onions, juniper berries, caraway seeds, and peppercorns. Reduce the heat to a low simmer, cover, and cook until the beer is infused with the flavor of the spices and the onions are completely wilted, about 45 minutes.

2 Prick the sausages with a fork on two sides and add them to the pot. Cover and simmer for 30 minutes. Meanwhile, preheat the grill to medium-hot (375°F on a gas grill).

3 Remove the sausages from the pot and immediately place them on the grill. Cook until browned and crispy on all sides, about 20 minutes.

4 Serve hot on frankfurter buns, topped with the beer-braised onions and plenty of spicy mustard.

SMOKED CHEDDAR BISCUITS WITH JALAPEÑO JELLY AND HAM

*From Robert Lyford, Patina Green
Home and Market, McKinney*

Chef Robert Lyford's smoked cheddar and ham biscuits are a regular sellout at Patina Green Home and Market. Neatly wrapped in butcher paper, they make a great breakfast snack while strolling around downtown McKinney's historic square. Patina Green stocks artisanal food products, like Leslie Luscombe's award-winning jalapeño jellies and Veldhuizen Family Farm's aged cheddars, alongside vintage furniture and home accessories. Each day Lyford gets fresh smoked ham from his McKinney neighbor Matt Hamilton at Local Yocal, a neighboring grocery specializing in grass-fed meats and local produce. An hors d'oeuvres tray of these delicious little biscuits are guaranteed to be a hit at any gathering.

Edible Tip

Lyford uses Luscombe Farm Jalapeño Peach Jelly.

FOR THE BISCUITS:
4 TSP SUGAR
2 TSP SEA SALT
2½ TSP BAKING POWDER
4¾ CUPS ALL-PURPOSE FLOUR
1½ STICKS (12 TBSP) COLD
   UNSALTED BUTTER, CUT INTO
   TABLESPOONS
1½ CUPS GRATED SMOKED
   CHEDDAR CHEESE
2 CUPS WHOLE MILK
1 EGG, BEATEN

TO ASSEMBLE:
1 (9 OZ) JAR SPICY FRUIT JELLY
1 LB SMOKED COUNTRY HAM,
   THINLY SLICED AND TORN INTO
   HALF-DOLLAR-SIZE PIECES

Makes 16–20 biscuits

MAKE THE BISCUITS:

1 Preheat the oven to 375°F. Line a baking sheet with parchment paper.

2 Sift together the sugar, salt, baking powder, and flour. Cut the butter into the flour using a pastry cutter until the mixture has the texture of small peas. Lightly mix in the cheese with a large fork. Add the milk all at once and stir with the fork until the mixture forms a ball.

3 Turn the mixture out onto a floured work surface and knead about 10 times, until a stiff dough forms. The dough should be dry enough so that it doesn't stick to your hands or the surface. You may need to add a pinch or two of flour to achieve this consistency. Roll the dough out with a floured rolling pin to a 1-inch thickness.

4 Cut with a 2-inch round cutter and place on a prepared baking sheet. Space out the biscuits to give them room to rise. With the scrap dough, you may repeat this procedure until all the dough is used. Brush the biscuits with the beaten egg and bake until the biscuits are golden brown, 14–17 minutes.

5 When the biscuits are cool enough to handle, slice them in half horizontally and place the tops to one side. Spread 2 teaspoons of jelly on each bottom half, and then place several pieces of ham on top of the jelly. Set the tops on the biscuits to complete the sandwich.

BEEVANGELISTS BRANDON AND SUSAN POLLARD

Texas Honeybee Guild, Dallas County

In an urban canyon shadowed by Dallas skyscrapers, a hive of happy honeybees lives on the terrace of the venerable Fairmont Hotel. The bees in chef André Natera's three-thousand-square-foot garden have been placed there courtesy of Brandon and Susan Pollard of the Texas Honeybee Guild. Walking through the garden with Natera on a hot July morning, the Pollards are happy to see a flurry of buzzing around a new patch of mint. There's ample fresh water in the solar-powered fountain and an assortment of nutrition: two types of mint, three kinds of basil, and pumpkin plants stretching across a nearby raised bed. The bees are in heaven.

These angels of agriculture so crucial to the health of the world's food supply have found their guardian angels in Brandon and Susan Pollard. For six years, the two have devoted themselves to spreading the word about bees. Thanks to volunteer sponsors, the Honeybee Guild has placed more than one hundred hives at residences, businesses, community gardens, and farms around Dallas County. The Pollards are a familiar sight at farmers' markets

and festivals, where Brandon, donning his bee suit with its bobbing antennae, patiently explains the inner workings of their glass-faced display hive.

There was a time when Brandon's life was devoted to defending a soccer goal. A member of the 1996 U.S. Olympic Soccer Team, Brandon was drafted out of the University of Virginia to play for the Dallas Burn. A devastating tackle shattered his leg in the closing moments of a 1999 playoff game. As the saying goes, when one door closes, another opens, and in flies something that changes your life.

On a breezy October day following his accident, Brandon was cooking in his apartment with the doors and windows open. Suddenly, there were bees. Lots of bees. But he didn't feel afraid—quite the opposite. The moment felt spiritual. The bees had found him, and over the next few weeks his fascination grew. Soon he joined the Collin County Hobby Beekeepers Association, and that's where he fell head over heels, not only for the bees but also for fellow member Susan, a holistic health-care practitioner who shared his passion. They became partners in marriage

and also in their mission to educate the public. They are self-proclaimed beevangelists.

"Bees are the litmus test for our environment," says Susan. "We talk about food deserts where people lack nutritious things to eat. The same is true for bees. You can build a beautiful organic garden, but if your neighbor contaminates his lawn and uses insecticides, your bees will pay the price. They travel between three and five miles in search of nectar."

To support their educational programs, the Pollards sell their Zip Code Honey, collected and labeled according to the neighborhood of its origin. About seven thousand pounds of honey are garnered by the Pollards annually in twenty of Dallas County's forty-three zip codes, and customers are encouraged to buy honey closest to their own neighborhood to help treat allergies, asthma, and other ailments.

"Honey is the cure in the cupboard," proclaims Brandon. "It was man's first sweetener, has natural preservatives, and age-old medicinal properties. It's an amazing and dynamic substance."

RESTAURANT AVA'S SMOKED PAPRIKA CHIVE MUFFINS

From Randall Copeland and Nathan Tate, Restaurant AVA, Rockwall

These melt-in-your-mouth buttermilk corn muffins, made with smoked paprika, chives, and local honey, are a staple at Restaurant AVA, where chefs Randall Copeland and Nathan Tate make all their breads in-house. Located in the lakeside community of Rockwall, Restaurant AVA features contemporary American cuisine with an emphasis on local ingredients. From the day they began planning the restaurant, they knew they wanted to develop long-lasting relationships with the folks producing their foods. They get their cheeses from Full Quiver Farms, their chicken from Windy Meadows Family Farm, and their produce from Barking Cat Farm, Eden Creek Farm, Truth Hill Farm, and Tom Spicer at Spiceman's FM 1410.

COOKING SPRAY
3 CUPS ALL-PURPOSE FLOUR
1½ CUPS YELLOW CORNMEAL
1¼ CUPS SUGAR
1 TBSP PLUS 1 TSP SALT
2 TBSP BAKING POWDER
1 TSP BAKING SODA
½ CUP LOCAL HONEY
½ CUP SOUR CREAM (NOT NONFAT)
3 LARGE EGGS
1⅔ CUPS BUTTERMILK
3½ STICKS (28 TBSP) UNSALTED BUTTER
2 TBSP OLIVE OIL
1 LARGE YELLOW ONION, CHOPPED
2 TBSP SMOKED PAPRIKA
¼ CUP CHOPPED FRESH CHIVES

Makes 3 dozen muffins

1 Preheat the oven to 350°F. Spray muffin tins with cooking spray. In a large bowl, sift together the flour, cornmeal, sugar, salt, baking powder, and baking soda. In a medium bowl, combine the honey, sour cream, eggs, and buttermilk and mix well.

2 In a small saucepan over low heat, melt the butter and let it simmer, stirring from the bottom regularly until it is golden brown. (It may foam slightly. Be careful not to let it burn—there is a fine line between brown and burned.) Remove from the heat and cover.

3 In a medium saucepan over medium-high heat, warm the olive oil. Add the onion and sauté until translucent gold, about 8 minutes. Transfer to a food processor and puree.

4 Make a well in the center of the flour mixture and add the honey mixture and onion puree. Fold together with a silicone spatula, just until no white streaks of flour remain. Add the brown butter, smoked paprika, and chives and stir to combine.

5 Fill the muffin pans three-fourths full with batter. Bake until the muffins are golden brown, about 20 minutes. Repeat with the remaining batter.

SWINE BLUE TACOS

From Jeana Johnson and Colleen O'Hare, Good 2 Go Taco, Dallas

At a small shopping center in East Dallas, there's a line out the door at Good 2 Go Taco. This gourmet taqueria is the brainchild of Jeana Johnson (Stephan Pyles, Hibiscus) and Colleen O'Hare (York Street, Green Room). "Our concept was to create a chef-driven restaurant that was accessible to everyone with daily quality and healthy choices," says O'Hare. "We knew from being in fine dining that restaurants, even those known for supporting local and sustainable, were only using the prime cuts and leaving the farmers with three-quarters of the animal. We wanted to be farmer friendly and turn those other cuts into delicious, creative tacos." One of their biggest hits has been the Swine Blue Taco, made with braised pork shoulder from Sloans Creek Heritage Meats. Their Red Wattle hogs, a Texas heritage breed, are known for their lean meat and rich flavor. The meat is slow-cooked until it is pull-apart tender and then wrapped in a warm tortilla with crunchy blue cheese slaw and creamy blue cheese dressing. Yum—so who said pork shoulder wasn't prime?

FOR THE PORK:

3 LB BONELESS PORK BUTT OR SHOULDER

2 TBSP KOSHER SALT, PLUS MORE TO TASTE

2 TBSP FRESHLY GROUND BLACK PEPPER, PLUS MORE TO TASTE

1 LARGE ONION, CUT INTO ¼-INCH-THICK RINGS

4 ROMA TOMATOES

2 JALAPEÑO CHILES

10 CLOVES GARLIC, PEELED

2–3 QUARTS STOCK (HAM OR CHICKEN)

FOR THE BLUE CHEESE VINAIGRETTE:

2 SHALLOTS, COARSELY CHOPPED

1 CUP RED WINE VINEGAR

2 TBSP DIJON MUSTARD

1½ CUPS OLIVE OIL

½ CUP CRUMBLED BLUE CHEESE

1 TSP KOSHER SALT

2 TSP FRESHLY GROUND BLACK PEPPER

FOR THE SLAW:

4 CUPS SHREDDED CABBAGE

½ CUP SHREDDED CARROTS

¼ CUP THINLY SLICED SCALLIONS

¾ CUP QUARTERED AND THINLY SLICED RADISHES

1 CUP LOOSELY PACKED FRESH CILANTRO LEAVES, CHOPPED

FOR SERVING:

6–8 TORTILLAS (CORN OR FLOUR)

½ CUP CRUMBLED BLUE CHEESE

Serves 6–8

MAKE THE PORK:

1 Preheat the grill to medium-high heat (400°F on a gas grill). Cut the pork into 1-pound pieces and sprinkle with the salt and pepper.

2 Lay the onion, tomatoes, and jalapeños on the grill and cook until charred but not burned, 2–3 minutes.

3 Put all of the grilled vegetables, along with the garlic, into a 5-quart Dutch oven. Cover and set aside at room temperature while grilling the pork.

4 Grill the seasoned pork for 16–20 minutes, turning to get a nice char on all sides, 4–5 minutes on each. Don't be afraid of the crispy black bits; they add flavor.

5 While the pork is grilling, preheat the oven to 275°F. When the meat is nicely charred, place the pork on top of the vegetables in the Dutch oven and add enough stock to cover the meat three-quarters of the way (this amount will vary depending on your cooking vessel). Cover the pot with foil, then the lid. Cook without peeking for 8 hours.

6 Remove from the oven and let cool until you can handle the meat without being burned. Pull off the pieces of excess fat and pull the meat apart. It will shred naturally. Taste the meat and correct the seasoning with salt and pepper if necessary.

MAKE THE VINAIGRETTE:

7 Place the shallots, vinegar, and mustard in a blender and pulse until the mixture is smooth. With the motor running on low speed, slowly drizzle in the olive oil and blend until the mixture is emulsified. Add the blue cheese and blend until fairly smooth. Season with the salt and pepper.

MAKE THE SLAW:

8 In a large bowl, combine the cabbage, carrots, scallions, radishes, and cilantro, and then dress with enough of the vinaigrette so that the slaw is wet but not saturated (you'll likely have vinaigrette left over). The slaw does not keep well and should be used as soon as it is mixed together.

ASSEMBLE THE TACOS:

9 Heat the grill to medium or prepare a nonstick griddle over medium heat. Heat the tortillas until each side is hot and a bit puffy. Reserve the tortillas under a cloth until all are warmed. In each tortilla, place a mound of pork, then a scoop of blue cheese slaw, and top with blue cheese crumbles. Serve immediately.

CHEESY BLONDE BREAD

From Adam and Robbie Werner, Stir Crazy Baked Goods, Fort Worth

Stir Crazy Baked Goods is a family-run business in Fort Worth that specializes in naturally made sweet treats using local and organic ingredients whenever possible. Owner Adam Werner learned to make beer bread from his now father-in-law when he was in college. "It was a great recipe for a student living on his own," says Werner. "It was quick, cheap, and a lot better tasting than the generic white loaf." Years later, his father-in-law had another insight to share. He'd heard about the Saturday tours at Rahr & Sons Brewing Company, so they went for a visit. "Their beers are exceptional," says Werner. "We've returned many times and our Cheesy Blonde Bread is the result." To create his bread, Werner pairs the Fort Worth–based brewery's Blonde Lager, a pale medium-bodied lager, with a tangy sharp cheddar. It's a recipe easy enough for a college kid and tasty enough for a grown-up gourmand.

BUTTER AND FLOUR FOR GREASING AND DUSTING THE LOAF PAN
3 CUPS ORGANIC ALL-PURPOSE FLOUR
¼ CUP SUGAR
1 TBSP NON-ALUMINUM BAKING POWDER
1 TSP GRANULATED SEA SALT

1 STICK (8 TBSP) SALTED BUTTER, MELTED
1½ CUPS PALE LAGER (RAHR & SONS BLONDE LAGER PREFERRED)
8 OZ SHARP CHEDDAR CHEESE, GRATED

Makes 1 loaf

1 Preheat the oven to 375°F. Lightly grease a 9 x 5-inch loaf pan with butter and dust with flour, tapping out the excess.

2 Combine the organic flour, sugar, baking powder, and salt in a large bowl. Pour in the melted butter, beer, and all but 2 tablespoons of the grated cheddar. Combine with a wooden spoon until everything is just moistened and no white streaks of flour remain.

3 Spoon the dough into the prepared loaf pan and sprinkle the remaining cheddar across the top. Bake until the loaf is golden brown on top and a toothpick inserted in the center comes out clean, 55–65 minutes.

Edible Tips

• Don't forget to grease and dust the loaf pan," says Werner. "I learned that trick from my wife, Robbie. Many of those college loaves ended up half stuck in the pans."
• Another Adam Werner suggestion—"You worked hard stirring. While waiting for the bread, utilize the remainder of the six-pack."
• The only readily available brand of non-aluminum baking powder is Rumford. Look for it in your local market.

UNCLE PAT'S FAVORITE POBLANO POT PIE

*From Kate Nelson, Piecurious Catering
and Pie Company, Dallas*

This Southwest-inspired pie is genuine comfort food. With a rich poblano cream gravy and farm-fresh ingredients, it's a homespun meal in a slice. Piecurious owner and Dallas native Kate Nelson names her pies after family members, either those who originated the recipe or those, like her Uncle Pat, who enjoy them most. Nelson learned about making chicken pot pie from her grandmother. "Whenever Mamaw cooked," says Nelson, "she wanted to get the maximum number of meals out of each dish, and a pot pie is a great way to extend the life of your leftovers. Don't be concerned about the vegetables or meats you use. These are the ones I use at Piecurious, but the gravy is the most important element. Be creative and throw in whatever you'd like."

2 (9-INCH) PIE CRUSTS
2½–3 CUPS CUBED LEFTOVER
  COOKED CHICKEN (FROM WHOLE
  ROASTED OR BOILED CHICKEN)
4 CARROTS, STEAMED OR BOILED
  UNTIL TENDER, DICED
½ CUP LEFTOVER COOKED GREEN
  PEAS
½ CUP LEFTOVER GRILLED CORN
  (CUT FROM THE COB)
½ CUP COOKED LIMA BEANS
5 TBSP OLIVE OIL
1 CLOVE GARLIC, MINCED
½ MEDIUM WHITE ONION, DICED

2 CUPS CHICKEN BROTH
⅓ CUP CORNSTARCH
3 TBSP FLOUR
2 CUPS HEAVY CREAM
4–5 POBLANO CHILES, ROASTED
  OR GRILLED, SKIN AND SEEDS
  REMOVED, CHOPPED
1 TSP SALT
1 TSP FRESHLY GROUND BLACK
  PEPPER
1 TSP CAYENNE

Serves 8

1 Preheat the oven to 350°F. On a lightly floured work surface, roll one pie crust flat to fit a 9-inch deep-dish pie plate. Press into the pie plate and set in the freezer. Roll the second piecrust out into a 10-inch circle. Use a thin metal spatula to place the crust on a sheet of plastic wrap. Cover with a second sheet of plastic wrap and place the flat, wrapped crust in the refrigerator while you assemble the filling.

2 Combine the chicken, carrots, peas, corn, and beans in a medium bowl; set aside.

3 In a small skillet over medium heat, heat 1 tablespoon of the olive oil and sauté the garlic and onion until pale gold and translucent, about 6 minutes. Set aside. In a 4-quart bowl, combine the broth and cornstarch; set aside.

4 In a large skillet, heat the remaining 4 tablespoons of olive oil over low heat, sprinkle in the flour, and cook, stirring constantly, for 3 minutes, to create a roux. Add the broth mixture, stirring continuously. Blend in the cream and poblanos and cook until well thickened, 2–5 minutes. Stir in the chicken-vegetable mixture and sautéed onion and garlic. Blend thoroughly, and then season with the salt, black pepper, and cayenne.

5 Remove the pie shell from the freezer and pour the hot filling into it. Remove the plastic wrap from the refrigerated crust, set on top of the filling, and seal the edge. Cut a few slits in the top crust. Bake until bubbling around the edges, 30–45 minutes. Transfer to a rack to cool for 10 minutes before serving.

TOM SPICER

Spiceman's FM 1410, Dallas

Peering in the doorway, you would be hard-pressed to identify FM 1410 as the leading edge of a food movement. Then again, you wouldn't take owner Tom Spicer for a culinary warrior. He isn't a chef, although his sister Susan Spicer is a famous one who plies her craft in New Orleans. He doesn't deconstruct or dabble in foam, although he's on the speed-dial of plenty of chefs who do. If you catch him in the right mood, he might sauté a mess o' mushrooms on a hot plate. But Spicer's not a kitchen man. He's a dirt man.

Whether he's recruiting local farmers to grow the special seeds he buys, cultivating high-demand items in his flourishing back-lot garden, or meeting a shipment of baby root vegetables from Baja at Dallas Love Field, Tom Spicer is a broker who's as passionate as his chefs are about well-cultivated produce and herbs.

Spiceman, as he's often called, is as New Orleans as Mardi Gras and gumbo. He grew up in the Crescent City and, after a stint at the University of Southern Louisiana, attended the elite Berklee College of Music in Boston. Music and food are his twin muses. With a little sweet-talking, he'll fire up the kalimbass, a combination of bass guitar and kalimba. Clarence "Gatemouth" Brown invited him to join his band, and later he toured as a bass man with Louisiana singer-songwriter Zachary Richard. It was Richard's girlfriend Claudette who introduced Spicer to the intoxication of French food in the early '80's, when the band was playing in Paris.

He likes to say his love of music comes from his dad, while his love of the land (the dirt) comes from his Danish mom, who taught him to garden. Connection to the soil runs deep in Spicer's family: his great-grandfather was an English horticulturist whom the Vanderbilts brought to New England in the early 1900s.

Spicer drifted toward produce gigs and moved to Dallas, where he eventually became the assistant produce manager at Bluebonnet, one of the city's seminal natural foods markets. "I was just a lettuce-and-herb guy at the time," he says and credits its Bluebonnet produce manager with teaching him the retail side of the business. Spicer also was mentored by Dallas produce icon Joe LaBarba, whom he says showed him how the Dallas Farmers Market worked. He was recruited by Golden Circle Farms, a job that converged with Dallas's first surge of interest in local sourcing. It was the 1980s, and regions across the country were taking Northern California's lead. At the time, Dallas helped birth southwestern cuisine.

"I was growing heirloom varieties [then]," Spicer says, "arugula, sprouts. I was selling baby arugula before California was selling it, four pounds for five dollars. We didn't call it heirloom, the specific varieties. We didn't call them microgreens."

There are those folks who poke their heads into FM 1410, look around, puzzle, and withdraw. There's nothing there as far as they can see. But for those curious enough to risk entry, it's a step into a unique universe where you won't get away without a farmer's-length conversation, a bag of something, and perhaps even an impromptu kalimbass performance.

CRÊPES SPICER

From Tom Spicer, Spiceman's FM 1410, Dallas

When Dallas urban farmer and produce broker Tom Spicer and his sister (New Orleans–based chef and cookbook author Susan Spicer) were growing up, one of their most eagerly anticipated meals was their Danish mom's Sunday morning crêpes suzette. But occasionally the parents' late-night Saturday parties meant the two youngest of their seven kids—Tom and Susan—had to forage for themselves the next morning. They figured out not just how to make their beloved crêpes, but even improved upon the recipe. In childhood, Tom's favorite filling was grape jelly, and he topped the crêpes with a flurry of powdered sugar and Froot Loops. These days, he uses seasonal fruit from his FM 1410 storefront, like Texas blueberries or fresh figs.

Edible Tip

To macerate fruit, cut it into bite-size pieces and toss with a little sugar in a bowl. Let stand at least 5 minutes.

1 CUP UNBLEACHED ALL-PURPOSE FLOUR
1 CUP WHOLE MILK
3 EGGS
2 TBSP BUTTER, MELTED, PLUS MORE FOR COOKING
PINCH OF SALT

3 CUPS MACERATED FRESH SEASONAL FRUIT, OR 2 CUPS LOCAL JAM, OR A COMBINATION
POWDERED SUGAR (OPTIONAL)

Serves 4 (makes about 12 crêpes)

1 Mix the flour, milk, eggs, melted butter, and salt together in a medium bowl. Strain out lumps through a sieve and let the batter stand for 5 minutes.

2 Meanwhile, preheat a crêpe pan or small nonstick skillet over medium heat for several minutes. Swirl a small pat of butter lightly over the bottom and sides of the pan, allowing it to froth slightly. Remove from the heat and pour 3 tablespoons batter into the pan, swirling to cover. Return the pan to the stove and cook the crêpe until the bottom side is a rich golden brown, 30–60 seconds.

3 Gently flip the crêpe over and cook for another 30 seconds, until it's brown and speckled. Set the crêpe aside on a plate and repeat the process until all 12 crêpes are cooked. As they come off the skillet, lay a sheet of parchment paper on each one as you stack them.

4 When all the crêpes are done, spoon a portion of macerated fruit or jam over each one, roll it up gently, and place it on a serving plate (3 crêpes per plate for adults). Dust each plate with powdered sugar, or garnish with a few dollops of jam or macerated fruit.

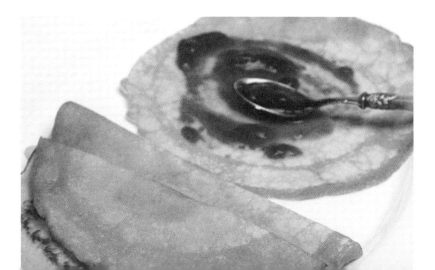

PEPPER JACK GRITS WITH CHORIZO AND EGG

*From Jill Lightner,
Edible Communities, Inc.*

It's hard to go wrong with stone-ground grits. The blended cooking liquid of chicken stock and whole milk creates a rich, flavorful base—and then we gild that lily with plenty of sausage and pepper jack cheese, for a dish that makes a great late-night supper or filling brunch. The poached eggs are designed to be cooked with runny yolks; stir the yolk into the grits for an extra layer of succulence. You can also skip the egg entirely for a delicious one-pot meal.

½ LB COOKED CHORIZO, REMOVED FROM CASINGS IF NECESSARY
2 CUPS CHICKEN STOCK
2 CUPS WHOLE MILK
1½ TSP KOSHER SALT
1 CUP STONE-GROUND GRITS
1 TBSP UNSALTED BUTTER

8 OZ PEPPER JACK CHEESE, COARSELY GRATED
4 LARGE EGGS
FRESHLY GROUND BLACK PEPPER

Serves 4

1 Crumble the chorizo into a medium saucepan set over medium-high heat. Cook, stirring, for 5 minutes. Add the stock, milk, and salt and bring to a low boil. Add the grits and reduce the heat to low. Cover and cook for 35–50 minutes, stirring often.

2 Once the liquid is completely absorbed and the grits are completely cooked, stir in the butter and cheese, remove from the heat, and stir until the cheese is melted. Cover the pot and set aside, keeping it warm.

3 Fill a small skillet with water. Set it over medium heat and bring the water to a rolling boil. Carefully crack the eggs into separate areas of the pan. Cook for 4 minutes; the yolks will have thickened but will still be fairly runny. Gently remove the eggs from the water with a slotted spoon and let sit on a plate until the water drains off.

4 Scoop a generous portion of chorizo and cheese grits into each of 4 small bowls. Top each portion with a poached egg and serve.

SPICY CORN, CRAB, AND BLACK BEAN SALAD

From Elissa Altman, Edible Communities, Inc.

A delicious salad that is chock-full of Texas staples, from black beans to jalapeños, this dish comes together in just a few minutes. If it's too hot to even think about turning on the stove, pick up cooked crab from a local market, toss the fresh ears of corn onto the grill, and open a can of black beans. It's also tasty served warm on corn tortillas; the mix of peppers, crisp red onion, fresh lime, and spices is versatile and just spicy enough to keep things interesting.

Edible Tips

◆ For a hit of more flavor and smokiness, grill the fresh corn before cutting it off the cob and adding it to the salad.
◆ Leftover cold boiled shrimp, removed from its shell and lightly chopped, can replace the crab in this recipe.

FOR THE DRESSING:
JUICE OF 1 LIME
¼ CUP NEUTRAL VEGETABLE OIL
¾ TSP ANCHO CHILI POWDER
½ TSP GROUND TOASTED CUMIN SEEDS
KOSHER SALT

FOR THE SALAD:
1½ CUPS COOKED CORN KERNELS

¾ CUP COOKED BLACK BEANS
1 LB BACKFIN OR LUMP CRABMEAT
½ RED BELL PEPPER, SEEDED AND DICED
1 SMALL TOMATO, CHOPPED
1 MEDIUM JALAPEÑO CHILE, DICED
1 SMALL RED ONION, DICED
¼ CUP FRESH CILANTRO, CHOPPED

Serves 4–6

MAKE THE DRESSING:

1 Whisk together the lime juice, oil, chili powder, and cumin. Season to taste with salt; set aside.

MAKE THE SALAD:

2 In a large glass bowl, combine the corn, beans, crabmeat, red pepper, tomato, jalapeño, onion, and half the cilantro. Add the dressing, toss well, and top with the balance of the cilantro.

3 Serve chilled, as is, or atop fresh tossed salad greens.

WILD BOAR POZOLE

*From Chris Hughes,
Broken Arrow Ranch, Ingram*

Pozole is a hearty southwestern stew that can be traced back to pre-Columbian Mexico. At the heart of the dish is hominy, a dried corn soaked in an alkaline lime solution. This ancient process, called *nixtamalization*, increases the corn's nutritional value and makes it easier to digest. Though domesticated pork can be used in this recipe, wild boar has a nutty, slightly sweeter taste, which nicely complements the earthy flavors of the chiles. It is estimated that more than two million wild boars (feral hogs) live in Texas, and their numbers are rapidly increasing, much to the dismay of many landowners. Given the animal's natural abundance, this free-range meat has been showing up more frequently on the menus of ecologically minded chefs. Broken Arrow Ranch, a Texas purveyor of wild game located in Ingram, ships USDA-inspected wild boar to home cooks and professional chefs around the world.

Edible Tip

To roast poblano chiles, set them in a rimmed baking pan and place them 2–3 inches under the broiler until the skins are charred, about 7 minutes. Flip them over and broil about 5 minutes longer, until the other side is charred. Remove from the oven and cover loosely with foil for 10 minutes. Remove skin, stems, and seeds. Rinse the chiles, and chop.

⅓ CUP CANOLA OIL
3 LB BONELESS WILD BOAR MEAT, CUT INTO 2-INCH CHUNKS, OR DOMESTICATED PORK (PREFERABLY SHOULDER OR LOIN), CUBED
¾ CUP UNBLEACHED ALL-PURPOSE FLOUR
3 QUARTS CHICKEN BROTH
2 (16 OZ) CANS HOMINY, DRAINED
1 LARGE ONION, CHOPPED
8 CLOVES GARLIC, MINCED
3 DRIED ANAHEIM CHILES, GROUND, OR 2 TBSP CHILI POWDER
2 POBLANO CHILES, ROASTED AND CHOPPED, OR 1 (7 OZ) CAN DICED GREEN CHILES, DRAINED
½ TSP DRIED MEXICAN OR REGULAR OREGANO
½ TSP FRESHLY GROUND BLACK PEPPER
SALT
CORN TORTILLAS
2 AVOCADOS, PEELED, PITTED, AND SLICED INTO 1-INCH WEDGES

OPTIONAL GARNISHES:
1 (8 OZ) CONTAINER SOUR CREAM
¾ CUP CHOPPED ONIONS
½ CUP FRESH CILANTRO, COARSELY CHOPPED

Serves 6–8

1 Heat the oil in a Dutch oven over medium-high heat until it shimmers. In a large bowl, lightly coat the meat with the flour, shaking off any excess. Add to the hot oil and brown on all sides in single-layer batches. Remove each batch as it is ready with a slotted spoon. When all the meat has been browned, deglaze the pot with a small amount of the broth, scraping up all the brown bits from the bottom of the pot.

2 Return the browned meat to the stew pot and add the hominy, onion, garlic, ground Anaheim chiles, poblano chiles, oregano, pepper, and remaining broth. Bring the mixture to a boil over medium-high heat. After several minutes, reduce the heat to low. Cover and gently simmer until the meat is fork-tender, about 2 hours.

3 Add salt to taste. Serve with corn tortillas and avocado slices. If you like, you can also top each serving with a spoonful of sour cream, chopped onions, and a sprinkle of cilantro.

CHILLED GAZPACHO WITH
HARISSA-MARINATED GRILLED GULF SHRIMP

*From Dean James Max, Asador,
Renaissance Dallas Hotel*

Like a dip in a cool pool, chilled gazpacho is the perfect antidote to the hot days of August in Texas. Made from refreshing cucumbers, lusty tomatoes, and a colorful assortment of peppers, this soup is a garden blend of summertime's best. To give it a little texture and pizzazz, chef Dean James Max adds one more Texas treasure to the mix—spicy morsels of grilled Gulf shrimp marinated overnight in a homemade harissa. Traditional harissa is a chile paste with North African roots, but this version, seasoned with a touch of cumin and jalapeños, has a definite Mexican flair. Gazpacho has long been linked to southern Spain, with its Moorish and Mediterranean influences, but the tomato (as well as the bell pepper and chile) was a New World plant. We have Columbus and his pals to thank for changing the color of this ancient soup to a hearty shade of red.

Note: Prepare the gazpacho and marinate the harissa shrimp the day before serving.

FOR THE GAZPACHO:

8 LARGE TOMATOES, QUARTERED
1 LARGE CUCUMBER, SEEDED AND
   COARSELY CHOPPED (PEELING IS
   OPTIONAL)
1 MEDIUM RED BELL PEPPER,
   SEEDED AND DICED
1 MEDIUM GREEN BELL PEPPER,
   SEEDED AND DICED
1 JALAPEÑO CHILE, SEEDED AND
   DICED
½ MEDIUM RED ONION, DICED
3 CLOVES GARLIC, SMASHED
1 CUP LOOSELY PACKED FRESH
   BASIL LEAVES
1 CUP LOOSELY PACKED CILANTRO
   LEAVES
1 TBSP GROUND CUMIN
2 TBSP SHERRY VINEGAR
¼ CUP EXTRA-VIRGIN OLIVE OIL
1 CUP DICED CIABATTA OR OTHER
   WHITE BREAD (CRUST REMOVED)

FOR THE SHRIMP:

1 CUP DICED PIQUILLO PEPPERS
2 TBSP CHILI SAMBAL
2 JALAPEÑO CHILES, SEEDED AND
   CHOPPED
2 CLOVES GARLIC, CHOPPED
1 TBSP GROUND CUMIN
1 TBSP GROUND CORIANDER
½ CUP GRAPESEED OIL
½ TSP TABLE SALT
6 OR 7 (10–12 COUNT) GULF SHRIMP,
   SHELLED AND DEVEINED
2 TBSP FRESH LEMON JUICE

TO FINISH THE GAZPACHO:

5 SHAKES OF TABASCO SAUCE
JUICE OF 2 LIMES (OR TO TASTE)
SALT
FRESHLY GROUND BLACK PEPPER
CHOPPED FRESH CILANTRO OR
   BASIL AND DRIZZLE OF OLIVE
   OIL FOR GARNISH (OPTIONAL)

Serves 6

MAKE THE GAZPACHO:

1 Combine the tomatoes, cucumber, bell peppers, jalapeño, onion, garlic, basil, cilantro, cumin, vinegar, olive oil, and ciabatta in a large nonmetallic bowl. Toss well to combine, cover, and let marinate in the refrigerator overnight.

MAKE THE SHRIMP:

2 Puree the piquillo peppers, chili sambal, jalapeños, garlic, cumin, and coriander in a blender or food processor. Once the mixture is fairly smooth and well mixed, slowly drizzle in the oil, and then add the salt.

3 In a large bowl, coat the shrimp with harissa marinade. Cover and refrigerate 20 minutes.

4 Preheat the grill to medium heat. Grill the marinated shrimp for several minutes on either side, just until the meat is opaque in the center. Sprinkle with the lemon juice. Dice. Cool the shrimp in the refrigerator for 15 minutes.

5 While the shrimp are cooling, puree the marinated gazpacho mixture in a blender (you'll probably have to do this in batches) until smooth. Add the Tabasco and lime juice and season to taste with salt and pepper.

6 Serve the gazpacho with a mound of diced shrimp in the center of the bowl. If you like, garnish with chopped cilantro or basil and drizzle with olive oil.

SPICY SWEET PECANS

From Jill Lightner, Edible Communities, Inc.

Usually glazed pecans show up around the holidays—and these are terrific in that role, handed around as a party snack or prettily packaged and handed out as gifts. But don't limit them to just that seasonal appearance. With fresh peaches and thick Greek yogurt, they make a tasty breakfast. Sprinkled on top of vanilla ice cream with dulce de leche, you've got a grand sundae. Chopped up and added to brownie batter, they turn plain old chocolate into a nicely spiced surprise. You can easily double the recipe, but if kept for more than a week, the nuts will lose some of their crunch.

¼ CUP GRANULATED SUGAR
¾ TSP GROUND CINNAMON
¼ TSP GROUND CLOVES
¼ TSP CAYENNE, OR TO TASTE
1½ TSP KOSHER SALT
2 TBSP UNSALTED BUTTER
2 TSP DARK BROWN SUGAR

2 TBSP TREATY OAK RUM OR
    OTHER SILVER RUM
2 TSP HONEY
4 CUPS UNSALTED ROASTED PECAN
    HALVES

Makes 1 quart

1 Line a baking sheet with parchment paper. Combine the granulated sugar, cinnamon, cloves, cayenne, and salt in a small dish; set aside.

2 Melt the butter in a medium saucepan over medium-high heat. While stirring, add the brown sugar, rum, and honey and bring to a boil. Add the pecans, stir to coat in the glaze, and continue cooking for about 2 minutes, until the nuts are shiny and completed coated in thick glaze.

3 Pour the glazed nuts onto the prepared baking sheet. Sprinkle on the sugar-spice mixture, and use a silicone spatula to coat the nuts in the mixture. Let cool to room temperature and store in an airtight container for up to 1 week.

SAVORY ZUCCHINI SOUP WITH PARMESAN AND LEMON ZEST

From Molly McCook, Ellerbe Fine Foods, Fort Worth

Every summer there is an abundance of squash in North Texas. "I love the bustle of the farmers' markets in the summer," says chef Molly McCook. "Every stand has some type of squash—zucchini, crook-neck, those unique Eight-Ball and One-Ball varieties. I also have a zucchini plant thriving in my backyard." So what do you do with all that squash? The chef suggests grilling it with a touch of Texas olive oil, salt, and pepper, or her favorite—cutting it into coins and sautéing it with onions and sprinkling it with Parmesan. You can also serve summer squash raw in salads or add it to your brownies. One more solution is this easy-to-prepare, savory soup that's delicious and beautiful whether served chilled or warm.

Edible Tip

Yellow squash, which is a bit sweeter, also works well in this recipe.

⅓ CUP OLIVE OIL
1 LARGE ONION, DICED
½ BUNCH SPRIGS FRESH THYME, TIED WITH A STRING
7 ZUCCHINI, CUT INTO ROUNDS (ABOUT 10 CUPS)
2 TSP KOSHER SALT, PLUS MORE TO TASTE
PINCH OF FRESHLY GROUND BLACK PEPPER, PLUS MORE TO TASTE
1 OZ FRESH BASIL LEAVES, CHOPPED
1 OZ FRESH FLAT-LEAF PARSLEY, CHOPPED

2 CLOVES GARLIC
1 QUART LOW-SODIUM VEGETABLE BROTH

FOR THE GARNISH:
ZEST OF 1 LEMON
FRESHLY GRATED PARMESAN CHEESE
EXTRA-VIRGIN OLIVE OIL

Serves 8

1 In a large sauce pot, heat the olive oil over medium heat. Add the onion and thyme bouquet and sauté until the onion is translucent. Add the zucchini rounds, salt, pepper, basil, parsley, and garlic. Continue to sauté over medium heat for about 5 minutes. Add the broth and bring to a simmer. Continue to cook until the zucchini begins to break down, about 25 minutes.

2 Remove from the heat and discard the thyme bouquet. Puree the soup until it's completely smooth, using an immersion blender and transferring it in batches to a regular blender. Taste the soup for seasoning and add more salt and pepper if desired.

3 Place 1 cup of soup in each of 8 soup bowls and garnish each serving with a sprinkle of lemon zest and Parmesan cheese and a drizzle of extra-virgin olive oil.

CELERY SOUP AND GULF CRAB SALAD ON WONTON CRISPS WITH A JALAPEÑO FOAM

From Jordan Swim, Vestals Foods and Food Creates Community, Allen

This beautiful soup presentation created by Jordan Swim features a crispy wonton with a mound of Gulf crab floating on a mild celery bisque. A peppery drizzle of jalapeño emulsion accents the dish. Swim and his wife, Emily, who shares his passion for food, began a venture in 2008 called Food Creates Community, a series of pop-up dinners featuring the products of local farmers and ranchers. They've taken their movable feast to various Dallas locations, including the Garden Cafe and Legal Grounds. Swim, who attended El Centro College's Culinary School, also owns a catering business, Vestals Foods, and teaches culinary arts at Allen High School.

FOR THE SALAD:
1 LB JUMBO LUMP GULF CRABMEAT
¼ CUP DICED CELERY
¼ CUP DICED RED ONION
¼ CUP CHOPPED FRESH CILANTRO
½ CUP HEAVY CREAM
JUICE AND ZEST OF 1 MEDIUM LIME
SALT
FRESHLY GROUND BLACK PEPPER

FOR THE JALAPEÑO EMULSION:
3 JALAPEÑO CHILES, HALVED, SEEDED, AND BLANCHED
⅓ CUP MILD OLIVE OIL
1 TBSP FRESH LIME JUICE

FOR THE WONTON CRISPS:
ABOUT 6 CUPS VEGETABLE OIL, FOR FRYING

8 SQUARE WONTON WRAPPERS, THAWED IF FROZEN
SALT

FOR THE SOUP:
2 TBSP COLD UNSALTED BUTTER, PLUS 1 TBSP UNSALTED BUTTER
5 CUPS CHOPPED CELERY
2 MEDIUM ONIONS, CHOPPED
1 (10 OZ) RUSSET POTATO, PEELED AND CUT INTO LARGE PIECES
4 CUPS CHICKEN STOCK, PLUS ADDITIONAL FOR THINNING THE SOUP
SALT
FRESHLY GROUND BLACK PEPPER
½ CUP HEAVY CREAM

Serves 8

MAKE THE SALAD:

1 In a medium bowl, combine the crab, celery, onion, and cilantro, tossing with a large fork or tongs to distribute the vegetables evenly. Pour the cream over the mixture, folding it in with a silicone spatula. Drizzle on the lime juice and sprinkle with the zest, and then season to taste with salt and pepper. Cover the bowl and chill the salad for at least 2 hours in the refrigerator. Just before assembling the final dish, taste and adjust the seasoning as desired.

MAKE THE JALAPEÑO EMULSION:

2 Puree the blanched jalapeños, olive oil, lime juice, and 2 tablespoons water in a blender until smooth. Transfer to a small bowl, cover, and let sit at room temperature until you assemble the final dish.

MAKE THE WONTON CRISPS:

3 Heat 1¼ inches of vegetable oil in a 4- to 5-quart Dutch oven over medium-high heat. Using a candy thermometer to gauge the temperature, heat the oil to 360°F.

4 Gently lay 2 wontons in the hot oil and fry, turning over once, until just golden, 15–30 seconds total. Transfer with a slotted spoon to paper towels to drain, and season with salt. Fry the remaining wontons in same manner. Set aside until the final assembly of the dish.

MAKE THE SOUP:

5 Melt 2 tablespoons of the butter in a large, heavy saucepan over low heat. Add the celery and onions, cover, and cook, stirring occasionally, until very tender, 15–20 minutes. Stir in the potato and add the stock. Cover, adjust the heat to medium-low, and simmer until all vegetables are very tender, about 30 minutes.

6 Puree with an immersion blender or transfer in batches to a regular blender. If needed, thin with more stock or thicken by reducing over medium heat. Season to taste with salt and pepper. Cover the pot, remove from the heat, and reserve, keeping warm, until the final assembly of the dish. Just before serving, stir in the cream and blend over medium heat. Turn off the heat and add the remaining 1 tablespoon of cold butter, stirring until it has completely melted.

ASSEMBLE THE DISH:

7 Ladle the hot soup into warm bowls. Scoop a mound of crab salad onto each wonton and float the wonton on top of the soup. Finally, drizzle the desired amount of jalapeño emulsion over the soup and crab wonton.

MAPLE CURRY ACORN SQUASH SOUP

From Brian C. Luscher,
The Grape, Dallas

Since 1972, The Grape has enchanted diners with its intimate tables, blackboard menu, and Left Bank ambiance. Chef Brian Luscher, who now owns the restaurant with his wife, Courtney, was a kid growing up in the Midwest when the Grape first opened its doors, but at fourteen he knew that he would someday become a chef. His grandfather and uncle owned a neighborhood restaurant and his dad was a butcher, who cooked for the family on Wednesday (his day off), with Brian by his side. A graduate of the Culinary Institute of America in Hyde Park, New York, Brian now rules the kitchen of this beloved Dallas establishment, while Courtney manages the front of the house. This velvety acorn squash soup with tones of maple, curry, and toasted cumin will transport your senses to a dreamy little bistro on a cobblestone side street of Paris.

Edible Tip

The Dallas Spice Market—also known as Kurry King—sells at several farmers' markets as well as online (DallasSpiceMarket.com). Its Madras curry powder is the perfect choice for this soup, with plenty of complex heat.

2–4 TBSP MADRAS CURRY POWDER
1 STICK (8 TBSP) UNSALTED BUTTER
3 ACORN SQUASH, HALVED AND SEEDED
3 TBSP CORN OR VEGETABLE OIL
1 MEDIUM YELLOW ONION, CHOPPED
3 CARROTS, CHOPPED
3 STALKS CELERY, CHOPPED
2 BAY LEAVES
1 TBSP GROUND CUMIN, TOASTED
2 CUPS CHARDONNAY

6 CUPS STOCK (CHICKEN RECIPE ON PAGE 58, OR VEGETABLE)
¼–½ CUP MAPLE SYRUP
JUICE OF 1 LEMON
¼ CUP CLOVER HONEY
2 CUPS HEAVY CREAM
SALT
FRESHLY GROUND BLACK PEPPER
CRÈME FRAÎCHE FOR GARNISH

Serves 8

1 Preheat the oven to 450°F. Combine the curry powder and butter in a small saucepan over low heat. Stir to blend as the butter melts. Remove from the heat once the butter has melted.

2 Place the squash halves on a sheet pan, cut side up. Baste each half with 1 tablespoon of the curry butter. Place in the oven and roast until fork-tender, about 25 minutes, basting lightly twice more during the process. Remove from the oven. When cool enough to handle, scoop the cooked squash from the shells and set aside.

3 Heat the oil in a stockpot over medium-high heat. When it begins to shimmer, add the onion, reduce the heat to medium, and cook until the onion is translucent, 5–7 minutes, stirring frequently. Stir in the carrots and the celery. When the carrots and onion begin to caramelize, about 5 minutes, add the bay leaves and cumin. Cook for 5 minutes; then add the cooked squash. Allow to cook for another 10–15 minutes, until the spices have become fragrant and the vegetables are well caramelized; you should see a dark brown crust forming in sections of the bottom of the pan.

4 Add the Chardonnay and deglaze the pan, scraping up the bits of brown crust. Increase the heat to medium-high and cook until the pan is nearly dry.

5 Add the stock and adjust the heat to high. Bring the stock to a boil and immediately reduce the heat to medium-low. Cook until all the vegetables are very tender; the squash should be basically disintegrated.

6 Remove from the heat, discard the bay leaves, and add ¼ cup of the maple syrup and the lemon juice, honey, and cream. Puree with an immersion blender or transfer in batches to a regular blender. Add salt, pepper and additional maple syrup to taste.

7 Divide the soup among 6 bowls, and garnish each serving with a dollop of crème fraîche. Serve immediately.

CHICKEN STOCK FROM STEWING HENS

*From Judi Glasgow,
JuHa Ranch, Barry*

In the winter, Judi Glasgow and husband Harry Butaud–their names form JuHa–cull their hen flocks. What happens to old hens? They're not good for roasting because they do get tough. But they can be delicious and tender if cooked in liquid. "That's why they're called stewing hens," says Glasgow, who also raises beef cattle, pigs, and lambs. The stock is worth waiting for—and freezing—as older hens have more flavor. "This liquid gold can get locavores through the winter, 'localizing' dried legumes that many soups are built around." Use the stock and cooked chicken to make stews, chicken and dumplings, and pasta casseroles. "I find adding the deboned meat at the last possible second to be the best for flavor," she says.

Edible Tip

Taste the stock during the last hour to monitor its progress. There's a big difference in the blended flavors and richness of a stock that has had a full simmer and one that hasn't.

1 (6 LB) STEWING HEN
2 MEDIUM ONIONS, QUARTERED
2 LARGE CELERY STALKS, WITH
   LEAVES
2 LARGE CARROTS, BROKEN INTO A
   COUPLE OF ROUGH PIECES
2 DRIED BAY LEAVES
2 SPRIGS FRESH THYME OR
   1 TSP DRIED THYME
10 BLACK PEPPERCORNS, OR
   MORE TO TASTE

Makes 4 quarts

1 Rinse the bird inside and out with water. Place it in a large stockpot with enough cold water to cover. It's okay if the leg tips are not submerged. Cover the pot and bring it to a boil over medium-high heat. Reduce the heat to low and simmer until the breast meat loosens from the bone, about 1½ hours. Every 30 minutes, remove the lid and skim any foam that forms on the surface.

2 Once the breast meat is falling off the bone, turn the heat off under the pot. Lift the chicken out and let it rest until it's cool enough to handle. Remove the meat from the bones and refrigerate for later use.

3 Return the bones and skin to the pot and add the onions, celery, carrots, bay leaves, thyme, and peppercorns. Set the heat to low and return the broth to a simmer for 2 hours.

4 Remove from heat and strain through a wide-mesh sieve into a clean pot. Allow the stock to cool completely to room temperature. Pack into 1-quart containers and either use immediately or freeze for later use.

PECAN LODGE SWEET POTATO BISQUE

From Diane and Justin Fourton,
Pecan Lodge Catering, Dallas

When that first blast of winter sweeps in from the west, this creamy bisque of autumn-harvested sweet potatoes will help warm both body and soul. Pecan Lodge has added a bit of southwestern fire to their version of this velvety southern soup. Chipotle chiles are smoke-dried jalapeños, brown and shriveled on their own, but when swimming in a dark-hued adobo sauce, they become soft and brick red. Add them to soups, stews, and vegetable dishes for a mildly spicy kick. Commercial versions, like La Costeña, can be found in the Mexican section of your grocer's, or you can make your own. Preserving chiles by drying them is a technique that dates back to pre-Columbian times. Diana Kennedy, the master of Mexican cuisine, has an authentic recipe for chipotle chiles in adobo sauce in her cookbook *My Mexico*.

FOR THE CHIPOTLE CREMA:
1 (7 OZ CAN) CHIPOTLE CHILES IN
    ADOBO SAUCE
1 CUP SOUR CREAM
1 TSP SALT

FOR THE BISQUE:
4 MEDIUM SWEET POTATOES
1 QUART HALF-AND-HALF
2 CUPS WHOLE MILK

1 TSP SALT
1 TSP GROUND CUMIN
¼ TSP ONION POWDER

GARNISH:
CHOPPED CHIVES OR CILANTRO
    (OPTIONAL)

Serves 4

1 In a food processor, puree the chipotles with the adobo sauce until smooth, and then strain through a wide-mesh strainer. Combine the sour cream and salt in a small bowl, and stir in 2½ teaspoons of the chipotle puree. (Reserve the remaining puree to adjust the spiciness of the soup to taste. Any puree left over can be frozen for later use.)

2 Preheat the oven to 425°F. Line a baking sheet with parchment paper.

3 Rinse the sweet potatoes, prick them in several places with a fork, and place them on the prepared baking sheet. Bake until the potatoes are completely soft, about 1 hour.

4 Cool the potatoes until you can handle them safely, and then cut them in half, remove the flesh from their skins, place in a medium bowl, and puree with an immersion blender until smooth. Pass the puree through a wide-mesh strainer to eliminate any remaining fibers.

5 In a Dutch oven or heavy stockpot, combine the sweet potato puree with the chipotle crema, half-and-half, milk, salt, cumin, and onion powder. Bring to a simmer and cook for about 15 minutes. For spicier soup, add more of the remaining chipotle puree.

6 Ladle the soup into bowls, garnish with a sprinkle of chives or cilantro, if desired, and serve immediately.

CHAPTER 3

SIDES

North Texas is a confluence of cultures.

The kitchens of Mexico and those of the South equally influenced our chuck wagons. We love our greens and cook them all sorts of ways, in a slow-simmer pot or in a casserole au gratin. We add them to risottos, lasagnas, and warm potato salads. Our fleeting spring offers asparagus for only a moment, and it's obvious how we treasure that vegetable by its appearance in three recipes here. We put fresh jalapeños in our Smokin' Beans and also add them to our very southern Corn and Okra Maque Choux. We love our traditional sweet potatoes but aren't afraid to venture away from customary recipes. Some things here are very familiar; some are a new spin on old favorites.

AUNT MABEL'S RUTABAGA CASSEROLE

From Beverly Thomas, Cold Springs Farm, Weatherford

Cold Springs Farm owner, Beverly Thomas, grew up in rural Mississippi, where her granny and her great-aunt Mabel taught her the finer points of southern cooking. "My great-aunt Mabel was a more educated cook than my granny," says Thomas, "and she cooked with more unusual ingredients—for instance, rutabagas instead of turnips. Like Granny, Aunt Mabel insisted on garden-fresh produce, and her husband Sidney obliged with a huge garden grown on a lot at the back of their house in Jackson. Reluctant city dwellers, they loved fresh vegetables." According to stories, Beverly's great-aunt Mabel was feeding her mashed green beans when she was only three months, which she believes partially explains her love for fresh vegetables. At her organic farm in Weatherford, Beverly Thomas grows both rutabagas and turnips, a fact that would make her granny and great-aunt Mabel very proud.

Edible Tip

Though it doesn't seem to make sense to dry the vegetables out and moisten them again later, Beverly Thomas says it's necessary—"Trust me, I have skipped this step and it definitely makes a difference!"

1 TSP SALT
1 TSP FRESHLY GROUND BLACK PEPPER
1 TBSP PLUS 1 TSP SUGAR
2 MEDIUM RUTABAGAS, PEELED AND CUBED
2 MEDIUM RED POTATOES, PEELED AND CUBED
½ STICK (4 TBSP) UNSALTED BUTTER
¾ CUP BUTTERMILK
1 EGG, SLIGHTLY BEATEN

Serves 4

1 In a 6- to 8-quart pot, combine 4 quarts water with the salt, pepper, and 1 tablespoon of the sugar; then add the rutabagas and potatoes. Cook over medium heat until the potatoes fall apart, 35–45 minutes. Drain, reserving about 1 cup of the cooking water.

2 Preheat the oven to 325°F. Butter a 2-quart casserole.

3 Using a hand mixer, whip the vegetables thoroughly until the mixture is fluffy and dry. If it's not dry, return to the pot and cook over low heat until it dries out. Add the remaining 1 teaspoon sugar, the butter, buttermilk, and beaten egg, and a little of the reserved rutabaga-potato water, and mix well. It should be slightly moist.

4 Pour the mixture into the prepared casserole and bake, uncovered, until the puree is puffy and golden brown, about 1 hour.

ASPARAGUS WITH BUTTER SAUCE

From Cynthia Chippendale,
Potager Cafe, Arlington

At Potager, Arlington's quirky, cool cafe, Cynthia Chippendale features daily chalkboard specials that reflect the season's freshest finds, like the spring asparagus she buys at the Downtown Arlington Farmers Market. "When you have wonderful fresh asparagus, you don't need to do much to make a delicious dish," says Chippendale. One of the unique aspects of Potager is its "pay what's fair" pricing policy. There are no set prices and people take only what they can eat. "No food gets wasted," says Chippendale. "This makes locally grown, nutritious food affordable for the average person." She is a firm believer in the tenets of Slow Food and was chosen to be a member of the U.S. delegation to Slow Foods' 2010 Terra Madre Conference, a biennial international gathering, in Turin, Italy.

2 LB FRESH ASPARAGUS
1 TBSP OLIVE OIL
SALT
FRESHLY GROUND BLACK PEPPER
JUICE OF 1 LEMON
1 STICK (8 TBSP) BUTTER, VERY COLD AND CUT INTO SMALL CUBES

1 TBSP CHOPPED FRESH HERBS (CHERVIL, CHIVES, AND PARSLEY ARE VERY NICE), OR MORE TO TASTE

Serves 4

1 Preheat the oven to 400°F.

2 Peel the tough ends of the asparagus (about 2 inches), but not the tender ends, and wash the spears well.

3 Lay the asparagus in a single layer on a baking sheet, drizzle with the olive oil, and season to taste with salt and pepper. Roast just until the spears are tender, but still crisp, 5–10 minutes. While the asparagus is roasting, make the butter sauce.

4 In a small saucepan, boil down the lemon juice until it is reduced by about half.

5 Remove from the heat and slowly add the butter, 1 cube at a time, whisking constantly until it is all incorporated. You will have a thick, emulsified lemon-butter sauce. Season to taste with salt and pepper.

6 Divide the asparagus among 4 plates, spoon the sauce over them, and sprinkle with the herbs.

SPINACH RISOTTO WITH GOAT CHEESE

From Graham Dodds, Hotel Palomar, formerly with Bolsa, Dallas

In this flavorful side dish, creamy risotto is blended with bright green spinach and earthy goat cheese. At Bolsa, the atmosphere is relaxed but full of panache. Located in a converted garage in the Bishop Arts District of Dallas, the restaurant is known for its farm-fresh ingredients like Caprino Royale's Bloombonnet goat cheese handcrafted in Waco, spinach from the Food for Good Farm at nearby Paul Quinn College, and local olive oil from the Texas Olive Ranch in Carrizo Springs.

FOR THE RISOTTO:
4½ CUPS CHICKEN STOCK
2 TBSP OLIVE OIL
1 TBSP UNSALTED BUTTER
1 LARGE YELLOW ONION, FINELY DICED
2⅔ CUPS ARBORIO RICE
½ CUP WHITE WINE
SALT
FRESHLY GROUND BLACK PEPPER

FOR THE SPINACH:
2 TBSP UNSALTED BUTTER
1 CLOVE GARLIC, MINCED
5½ OZ SPINACH, HEAVY STEMS REMOVED

FRESHLY GRATED NUTMEG
SALT
FRESHLY GROUND BLACK PEPPER

TO FINISH THE RISOTTO:
¾ STICK (6 TBSP) UNSALTED BUTTER
½ CUP FRESHLY GRATED PARMESAN CHEESE
SALT
FRESHLY GROUND BLACK PEPPER
8 OZ TEXAS BLOOMBONNET GOAT CHEESE, CRUMBLED

Serves 8

1 In a large pot, bring the stock to a boil and reduce the heat to a simmer.

2 In another large pot, heat the olive oil over medium heat. Add the butter; then sauté the onion until soft but not browned, about 10 minutes. Add the rice and turn up the heat to medium-high. Stir constantly, until the rice is completely coated with oil. Add the wine, stirring until it has been completely absorbed by the rice. Reduce the heat to medium and add the hot stock one ladle at a time, stirring the rice continually and waiting until the liquid is absorbed before adding the next ladle.

3 Lower the heat and cook slowly. It will take about 30–35 minutes for the rice to become al dente. Leave the pot sitting on the burner with the flame turned off while you prepare the spinach mixture.

MAKE THE SPINACH MIXTURE:
4 Melt the butter in a medium saucepan over medium heat. Add the garlic and spinach. Grate in about an eighth teaspoon of fresh nutmeg. Sauté until the spinach wilts. Remove from the heat and season with salt and pepper to taste. Put the spinach mixture in a food processor and puree. Taste for seasoning and add salt and pepper as needed.

FINISH THE RISOTTO:
5 Blend the spinach puree, along with the butter and Parmesan, into the rice, and season to taste with salt and pepper. Sprinkle the crumbled Bloombonnet on top and serve immediately.

PAULA LAMBERT

The Mozzarella Company, Dallas

After three decades, Paula Lambert still talks about cheese and her Mozzarella Company with the exuberance of a new business owner. When asked which of her twenty-plus cheeses is best suited for stuffing squash blossoms, she quickly extols the virtues of her Oaxacan queso blanco, a crumbly, white cow's milk cheese with flecks of the Mexican herb epazote and zesty bits of green jalapeños. Years ago, she learned the finer points of making it when she traveled to Mexico to work with native cheese artisans. Her quest to learn from the best has led her on a journey that has taken her all over the world.

Mozzarella was her first love. She acquired a taste for it in the Umbrian town of Perugia, where she moved to study art history and Italian. What began as a youthful adventure turned into a five-year stay that altered her life's direction. She returned to the States in 1973, married, and resettled in Dallas, but the Italian lifestyle, with its village markets, local wines, and fresh foods, had already cast its spell. She longed for a business that combined her two passions: Italy and cooking. Her lightbulb moment came on a return trip to visit Italian friends. During a leisurely lunch that included tomatoes and fresh moz-

zarella, she realized that no one in Texas was making this cheese that she loved. Two of her girlfriends helped with seed money, and the Mozzarella Company was born.

In 1982, there were only a handful of artisan cheese makers in the United States. Paula returned to Italy to learn the skill of mozzarella making and

hired an Italian cheese maker to come to Dallas to help set up the operation. In spite of the hard work and a quality product, the American consumer wasn't ready, and sales in the beginning years were not what she'd hoped.

Enter a group of innovative young chefs—Stephan Pyles, Dean Fearing, and Robert Del Grande—experiment-

ing with their southwestern version of the New American cuisine. They convinced her to add chiles and local herbs to enhance her cheeses. She traveled to Italy, Greece, France, and Mexico and began making new varieties.

The orders finally began coming in from local chefs and chefs in other parts of country, like Chicago's Rick Bayless, who appreciated Paula's attention to authenticity. With a new cuisine being celebrated, the American public finally caught up, and sales skyrocketed. The Mozzarella Company has continued to grow, in large part because of Paula's tenacity and positive approach to both business and life.

Her eighteen employees, several of whom have been with her for decades, still craft Mozzarella Company cheese by hand. Paula buys her milk from regional dairies and the herbs from local farms. She is a fierce defender of Texas farmers and is excited about the growing number of new artisan cheese makers. A true pioneer of the American culinary world, she was inducted in 1998 into the James Beard Foundation's Who's Who of Food and Beverage in America. And even now, after two cookbooks, a stack of awards, and countless gallons of milk, she still speaks about cheese with a gleam in her eye.

ROASTED BEETS, FETA, AND FRISÉE SALAD

From Paula Lambert, The Mozzarella Company, Dallas

The Mozzarella Company sells more than twenty types of fresh and aged cheeses made from cow's milk and goat's milk. Since 1982, owner Paula Lambert has traveled to the villages of Italy, Greece, Mexico, and France to learn the age-old methods of cheese making. "I learned to make Greek feta in the mountain village of Metsovo," says Lambert. "We visited shepherds who were also cheese makers. They made their feta in a tiny hut. The fresh milk was chilled with water from a rushing stream and later heated over a wood fire for cheese making." In this beet and feta salad, she pairs earthy-tasting sweet beets with the sharp and salty tang of feta. Both are tossed in a lemon-dill dressing and piled high on a bed of frisée lettuce. Says Lambert, "I love how the beets stain the feta to pink."

FOR THE BEETS:
2 LB SMALL FRESH BEETS
¼ CUP EXTRA-VIRGIN OLIVE OIL
SALT
FRESHLY GROUND BLACK PEPPER

FOR THE DRESSING:
¼ CUP FRESH LEMON JUICE
½ CUP EXTRA-VIRGIN OLIVE OIL
¼ CUP CHOPPED FRESH DILL
1 TSP GRATED LEMON ZEST
1 TSP GRATED ORANGE ZEST

FOR THE SALAD:
4 OZ FETA CHEESE, CRUMBLED
   (½ CUP)
1 TBSP CRACKED BLACK
   PEPPERCORNS
1 LARGE HEAD FRISÉE LETTUCE,
   SEPARATED INTO LEAVES,
   WASHED, AND SPUN DRY
FRESHLY GROUND BLACK PEPPER

Serves 8–10

ROAST THE BEETS:
1 Preheat the oven to 350°F. Then wash the beets and trim the stem ends to 1 inch. Peel the beets and cut them into quarters. Coat with the olive oil and sprinkle with salt and pepper. Lay the beets in a shallow roasting pan just large enough to hold them in a single layer. Tightly cover with aluminum foil. Place in the oven and roast until tender, about 1 hour. Remove from the oven, loosen the foil, and place on a rack to cool. When cooled, transfer the beets to a bowl.

MAKE THE LEMON-DILL DRESSING:
2 Whisk the lemon juice, olive oil, dill, and zests together in a small bowl.

ASSEMBLE THE SALAD:
3 Pour half the dressing over the beets when they have cooled. Toss to combine. Then sprinkle the feta and cracked pepper over the beets. Toss to combine.

4 When ready to serve, tear the frisée into bite-size pieces and place in a bowl. Pour the remaining dressing over the frisée and toss to coat well. Transfer the lettuce to a serving dish and mound the beets and feta on top. Grind additional pepper over the salad. Serve at room temperature.

ASPARAGUS GREMOLATA WITH GINGER RICE

From Cosme Alcantar, Blue Mesa Grill, five locations in the Dallas & Fort Worth Metroplex

Springtime in Texas is a painfully fast affair, barely a memory as temperatures change from bitter cold to stifling heat in no time flat. Perhaps that's why we appreciate the season all the more, getting nearly giddy when baskets of spring asparagus begin cropping up at local markets. Those wanting to savor this local gem should arrive early; farmers sell out quickly. At Blue Mesa Grill, known for its commitment to local produce, executive chef Cosme Alcantar serves steamed asparagus with a topping of festive gremolata, speckled with the zest of Texas grapefruits and oranges. Coconut-flavored rice seasoned with basil pesto and bits of pickled ginger completes the plate, a beautiful expression of our brief seasonal fling with spring.

FOR THE GREMOLATA:

¼ CUP FLAT-LEAF PARSLEY, FINELY CHOPPED

¼ CUP FINELY CHOPPED FRESH CILANTRO

1 TBSP GRATED GRAPEFRUIT ZEST

1 TBSP GRATED ORANGE ZEST

2 TBSP MINCED GARLIC

FOR THE GINGER RICE:

2 TBSP UNSALTED BUTTER

1 TBSP CHOPPED PICKLED GINGER

1 TBSP MINCED GARLIC

¼ CUP DICED YELLOW ONION

1 CUP WHITE RICE

¼ CUP UNSWEETENED COCONUT MILK

½ TSP KOSHER SALT

PINCH OF WHITE PEPPER

½ TBSP PREPARED BASIL PESTO

FOR THE ASPARAGUS:

1 LB ASPARAGUS, 1–2 INCHES TRIMMED OFF THE BOTTOMS

Serves 4

MAKE THE GREMOLATA:

1 In a medium bowl, combine the gremolata ingredients and set aside.

MAKE THE GINGER RICE:

2 Melt the butter in a medium saucepan over medium heat. Add the ginger, garlic, and onion; stir frequently, cooking until the onion is transparent. Add the rice, turning frequently until well coated with the butter. Add the coconut milk, 2 cups water, and the salt and pepper, and bring to a boil. Reduce the heat to low, cover, and simmer about 20 minutes. Remove from the heat and let stand 5–6 minutes. Right before serving, turn the cooked rice into a serving bowl, add the pesto, and toss with a fork to fluff and distribute flavor.

COOK THE ASPARAGUS:

3 Place the asparagus spears in a wide skillet with enough water to cover or in a steaming basket over 1 inch of water. Bring to a rapid boil over high heat. Reduce the heat to medium and cook until the ends of the spears are tender but still slightly resistant when pierced with a fork, 3–5 minutes. Remove the asparagus from the pot and rinse under cool water to stop the cooking process.

4 Top each portion (about 4 or 5 spears) with 2 teaspoons of the gremolata. Serve with the ginger rice and Blue Mesa's Orange Sriracha-Glazed Chicken (page 99).

WARM ROASTED POTATO, BACON, AND BLUE CHEESE SALAD

From Chad Houser and Janice Provost, Parigi, Dallas

Chefs Chad Houser and Janice Provost elevate humble potato salad with the addition of fresh herbs, scallions, applewood-smoked bacon, and Paula Lambert's Deep Ellum Blue cheese. Houser and Provost are co-owners of Parigi, an upscale Dallas bistro with a menu full of locally grown products. One of the resources the duo relies on is Dallas County Youth Village, a juvenile detention facility for nonviolent adjudicated young men. Here students maintain twelve raised beds for their culinary arts program. Houser and Provost are the driving force behind a new initiative called Café Momentum, a series of monthly pop-up dinners created to benefit the Youth Village's budding young chefs. Hopes are to raise enough funds to give Café Momentum a permanent home.

1 LB NEW POTATOES, CUT INTO QUARTERS
1 TSP CHOPPED FRESH ROSEMARY
1 TSP CHOPPED FRESH THYME
1 CLOVE GARLIC, MINCED
2 TBSP EXTRA-VIRGIN OLIVE OIL
1½ TSP KOSHER SALT
1½ TSP FRESHLY GROUND BLACK PEPPER
½ CUP CHOPPED APPLEWOOD-SMOKED BACON, COOKED CRISP AND DRAINED
¼ CUP CHOPPED SCALLIONS
6 OZ BLUE CHEESE, CRUMBLED
2 TBSP BALSAMIC VINEGAR

Serves 4

1 Preheat the oven to 350°F. Line a baking sheet with parchment.

2 Place the potatoes in a large bowl and toss together with the rosemary, thyme, garlic, olive oil, salt, and pepper. Place on the prepared baking sheet and roast until evenly golden brown and soft on the inside, about 45 minutes.

3 Transfer the hot potatoes to a mixing bowl and toss with the bacon, scallions, blue cheese, and vinegar. Serve warm.

BRAISED SOUTHERN GREENS

*From Jon Bonnell, Bonnell's,
Fort Worth*

The unique aroma of braising greens fills many southern kitchens as well as the childhood memories of many Texans. There are so many different types of sturdy, hearty greens to choose from, including collards, beet greens, mustard greens, and kale. Chef Jon Bonnell suggests combining three or four varieties for complexity and balance. Be sure to wash all greens thoroughly and plunge them deep into cold water to remove any sand. The tough stems of most greens, though flavorful, are too fibrous and stringy to enjoy in this dish, so it's best to discard them. Serve with pepper vinegar or hot sauce for an extra little kick.

4 SLICES BACON, DICED
½ SMALL ONION, DICED
4 CLOVES GARLIC, MINCED
2 LB GREENS (TURNIP, MUSTARD, AND BEET GREENS, CHARD, AND COLLARDS ALL WORK WELL), CLEANED OF ANY DIRT OR SAND, STEMS REMOVED, AND LEAVES COARSELY CHOPPED

1½ TSP KOSHER SALT
½ TSP FRESHLY GROUND BLACK PEPPER
¼ CUP DRY WHITE WINE
2 TBSP APPLE CIDER VINEGAR

Serves 4

1 Place a large stockpot over medium heat, add the bacon, and cook until most of the fat has been rendered, about 8 minutes. Add the onion and garlic and cook, stirring a few times, until the onion is soft and translucent, about 8 minutes.

2 Add the chopped greens to the pot along with the salt and pepper; then pour in the wine. Cover and reduce the heat to low. Cook until the greens have cooked down and are tender, 15–20 minutes.

3 Remove the lid and stir in the vinegar just prior to serving.

BUTTERNUT SQUASH LASAGNA

*From Eric Hunter, Fire Oak Grill,
Weatherford*

Using butternut squash as an alternative to pasta in lasagna was an experiment that paid off for chef Eric Hunter. This dish has been a real hit at Hunter's Fire Oak Grill in historic downtown Weatherford. Creating new dishes from seasonal, locally grown ingredients is something he's passionate about, though he does have a secret advantage over his city peers. Less than a quarter mile from his home, Beverly Thomas at Cold Springs Farm grows an array of organic fruits and vegetables, including heirloom and rare varieties. A native of Fort Worth, Hunter got his early training from his dad, a competitive chuck wagon cook. He and his wife, Jennifer, met while working at chef Tim Love's Lonesome Dove Western Bistro, he as chef de cuisine and she as the general manager. Wanting to slow down and enjoy small-town life, Hunter helped open Fire Oak Grill in 2007 and the couple was able to purchase the restaurant in 2010.

FOR THE TOMATO SAUCE:

1 TBSP OLIVE OIL

1 SMALL YELLOW ONION, ROUGHLY CHOPPED

8 CLOVES GARLIC, MINCED

1 CUP WHITE WINE

5 LARGE TOMATOES, ROUGHLY CHOPPED

2 TBSP CHOPPED FRESH BASIL

1 TSP CHOPPED FRESH OREGANO

SALT

FRESHLY GROUND BLACK PEPPER

FOR THE LASAGNA:

3 LARGE BUTTERNUT SQUASH (ABOUT 6 LB TOTAL)

½ CUP OLIVE OIL FOR BRUSHING ON SQUASH AND WILTING SPINACH

SALT

FRESHLY GROUND BLACK PEPPER

2 LB FRESH SPINACH LEAVES, HEAVY STEMS REMOVED

4 CUPS SHREDDED MOZZARELLA CHEESE

Serves 6–8

MAKE THE TOMATO SAUCE:

1 Heat the oil in a medium saucepan over medium heat until warm; then add the onion and garlic and cook, stirring, until they are pale gold. Add the wine and cook until reduced by half. Add the tomatoes and herbs and cook until the liquid starts to thicken. Puree the sauce, in batches, in a blender until chunky but spreadable. Season with salt and pepper.

MAKE THE LASAGNA:

2 Preheat the over to 350°F. Line 2 baking sheets with parchment paper. Peel and seed the butternut squash. Slice into pieces 1/16 inch thick (a mandolin works best) and transfer to the prepared sheets. Brush the slices with a generous 2 tablespoons of the oil, and season with salt and pepper. Bake until tender and fully cooked, 15–20 minutes. Remove from the oven, but leave the oven set to 350°F.

3 While the squash cooks, heat the remaining oil in a large sauté pan over high heat until slightly smoking. Add the spinach and sauté briefly, until wilted. Remove from the heat and cool. Drain it in a colander and press out the liquid.

4 Cover the bottom of a lightly greased 9 x 13-inch lasagna pan with a layer each of spinach and squash slices. Spread 2/3 cup tomato sauce evenly over the top, and then sprinkle with 1 1/3 cups cheese. Repeat this process two more times, ending with a layer of cheese. Press down the lasagna firmly and bake, uncovered, until all the cheese is melted, 10–15 minutes. Remove from the oven and let cool 10 minutes before serving.

CELEBRATION'S SAUTÉED KALE

*From John Stout, Celebration
Restaurant, Dallas*

Kale is a super food, and no restaurant does it better than Dallas's Celebration Restaurant. Although kale appears to be a tough green in need of protracted cooking and stewing, chef John Stout says that it's actually best prepared with a quick sauté. Overcooking can cause it to lose its gorgeous color and turn bitter. Cooked al dente, it retains its fresh taste. Since 1971, Celebration Restaurant has been cooking up home-style meals in its little stone cottage, which has grown to include more dining rooms, an expansive patio, a catering company, and a food-to-go market.

Edible Tip

A great variation on this dish is to omit the cranberries and walnuts and instead add 2 teaspoons sesame seeds to the sauté pan along with the soy sauce.

2 TBSP OLIVE OIL
1 CLOVE GARLIC, MINCED
2 LB FRESH KALE, RINSED WELL
   AND STEMS REMOVED
2 TBSP DRIED CRANBERRIES

2 TBSP COARSELY CHOPPED
   WALNUTS
1 TBSP SOY SAUCE
½ TBSP KOSHER SALT

Serves 4

1 Preheat a large skillet over high heat. Add the olive oil, then sauté the garlic for about 30 seconds. Add the kale, cranberries, walnuts, soy sauce, and salt, and sauté just until the kale is al dente, 3–4 minutes. Serve immediately.

PECAN LODGE COLLARD GREENS GRATIN

From Justin and Diane Fourton, Pecan Lodge Catering, Dallas

Fixin' a mess of greens is a southern tradition. Eating those greens on New Year's Day with black-eyed peas and corn-bread will guarantee you prosperity or, at the very least, add a powerful punch of nutrition to your diet. A pot of collard, mustard, or turnip greens slow-cooked with a slab of salt pork or ham hocks is classic southern comfort food, chock-full of vitamins, iron, and calcium. Collards, a cousin of kale and cabbage, grow in loose bunches and are at their peak in the middle of the winter. Their broad, bluish green leaves are mild and slightly bitter.

Southern cuisine is a specialty of Pecan Lodge Catering, located at the Dallas Farmers Market. This gratin is a special-occasion casserole for family gatherings or when company comes calling. It's rich and creamy and has a layer of French-fried onions on top—you know, the ones you eat by the handful when no one's looking?

Edible Tips

• *Chiffonade* is a French term for slicing the leaves of vege-tables into thin strips. Stack several collard leaves and roll into a tight cylinder. With a sharp knife, slice crosswise into ⅛-inch-wide strips.

• If desired, you can assem-ble the casserole up to 2 days ahead and refrigerate. Before baking, let sit at room temperature for 30 minutes.

1 CUP DICED BACON
¾ CUP DICED RED ONION
1 CUP SLICED BABY PORTOBELLO
   MUSHROOMS
2 BUNCHES COLLARD GREENS,
   RINSED WELL, DEVEINED, AND
   CUT INTO A CHIFFONADE
5⅓ TBSP UNSALTED BUTTER
⅓ CUP UNBLEACHED ALL-PURPOSE
   FLOUR
2½ CUPS HEAVY CREAM
SALT
FRESHLY GROUND BLACK PEPPER
¾ CUP GRATED ASIAGO CHEESE
½ CUP CANNED FRENCH-FRIED
   ONIONS

Serves 6–8

1 Preheat the oven to 350°F. Butter an 8 x 12-inch casserole dish (or 2- to 2½-quart casserole).

2 In a large frying pan or Dutch oven, fry the bacon over medium heat until it is half-cooked (the white will be opaque, but the meat not yet crispy). Add the red onion and mushrooms and sauté until the bacon is fully cooked and the onion has softened.

3 Increase the heat to high, add the collard greens in batches, and cook until the greens are wilted. Turn off the heat and set aside.

4 In a separate pan, melt the butter over medium heat; then add the flour. Cook, whisking frequently, to create a smooth, blond roux (this will take 3–4 minutes; do not brown). Slowly add the cream while whisking. Adjust the heat to keep the sauce at a simmer. Add salt and pepper to taste (it should taste like a moderately salty cream gravy). Continue cooking until the sauce thickens and easily coats the back of a spoon.

5 Combine the collard greens with the cream sauce and transfer to the prepared casserole. Top with the cheese and fried onions. Bake, uncovered, until cooked through, about 30 minutes.

CORN AND OKRA MAQUE CHOUX

From Beverly Thomas, Cold Springs Farm, Weatherford

Beverly Thomas's love for the land can be traced back to her Mississippi childhood. "My grandparents had a huge garden next to the house," remembers Thomas. "I always looked forward to spring, when my grandfather hired Mr. Paul to come and plow up the garden with our mule Chester. I'd sit in the mimosa tree next to the garden and watch. After a while, he'd feel sorry for me and let me ride Chester while he plowed." Her grandmother made memorable Sunday dinners from the things they grew. "Granny served a version of this recipe, but I've made a few alterations. Fresh vegetables are important for this to turn out right. Fresh corn has more starch. It's the corn's browned starches that give it an authentic southern flavor." Today, Thomas uses sustainable methods to grow her own sweet corn, tomatoes, and okra at Cold Springs Farm in Weatherford.

Edible Tip

Using farm-fresh eggs will make all the difference in the taste of this recipe. Thomas loves the bright yellow color and rich flavor of the yolks.

¼ CUP OLIVE OIL
1 CUP FRESH OKRA, SLICED
½ STICK (4 TBSP) UNSALTED BUTTER, SOFTENED
3½ CUPS FRESH WHITE SWEET CORN KERNELS CUT OFF THE COB
3½ CUPS FRESH YELLOW SWEET CORN KERNELS CUT OFF THE COB
½ CUP CHOPPED SWEET YELLOW ONION
½ CUP CHOPPED RED ONION
1 CUP MIXED CHOPPED RED AND GREEN BELL PEPPER

3 SERRANO CHILES, FINELY CHOPPED (OPTIONAL)
1½ TSP KOSHER SALT
1 TSP FRESHLY GROUND BLACK PEPPER
1 TSP SMOKED SWEET PAPRIKA
1 LARGE BAY LEAF
1 CUP CHICKEN STOCK
2 FARM-FRESH EGGS, BEATEN
1 CUP BUTTERMILK
¼ CUP SUGAR

Serves 4-6

1 In a heavy large Dutch oven or deep cast-iron skillet, heat the olive oil over medium-high heat. Add the okra and brown it. Add the butter, corn, onion, bell pepper, chiles, salt, pepper, paprika, bay leaf, and stock.

2 Increase the heat to high and cook until the butter melts and the liquid in the pot comes to a boil. Stir and scrape the bottom of the pan occasionally to mix in the browned scrapings (the starches from the corn). Cover and let cook for 3 minutes without stirring to allow more of the corn's starches to brown. Scrape and stir and continue cooking until the onion is tender.

3 Remove the bay leaf. Reduce the heat to medium-high and continue cooking until the mixture really sticks to the bottom of the pan, about 10 minutes. Stir and scrape as needed. Reduce the heat to low.

4 In a small bowl, stir together the eggs and buttermilk until frothy; then slowly add to the corn mixture, stirring all the while so the eggs don't get too hot and cook. Once the egg mixture is thoroughly mixed in, raise the heat to medium-high and bring to a boil, stirring and scraping the bottom a few times. Stir in the sugar, reduce the heat to low, and cover. Simmer until the corn is cooked, about 15 minutes. Stir and scrape the bottom just enough to keep the mixture from sticking (browned is good, burned is not). Serve hot from the stove top.

KATY'S GRILLED BALSAMIC PEACHES

From Katy Lopez, chef contributor to
Edible Dallas & Fort Worth

Nothing quite matches the sensory experience of biting into a ripe peach: the sweet fragrance, the dense, almost creamy texture, and the sticky dribble of juices. More than a million peach trees grow in Texas, and North Texas is home to many of those orchards. From May into July, local peaches are on display at roadside stands, farmers' markets, and grocers. Varieties of flesh tones range from a creamy yellow to orange blush. To avoid bruising, test the fruit for ripeness at the top curve where it was attached to the stem. When gently pressed, the area should be soft to the touch, though not overly so. It should also smell like a peach—summery and fresh. In this recipe, grilling adds a layer of caramelized flavor to the fruit's natural sweetness. Serve it as a side dish beside your favorite meat.

½ CUP BALSAMIC VINEGAR
1 TBSP HONEY, WILDFLOWER OR
   OTHER LOCAL VARIETY
2 TBSP LIGHT BROWN SUGAR
1 TSP FRESHLY GROUND BLACK
   PEPPER

⅛ TSP SALT
4 RIPE PEACHES, HALVED AND
   PITTED

Serves 4

1 Mix together the vinegar, honey, brown sugar, pepper, and salt in a small saucepan and bring to a simmer over medium heat, 2–3 minutes. Place the peach halves in a medium bowl and pour the vinegar glaze on top. Let sit for 15–20 minutes.

2 Preheat the grill to medium-high heat. (You can also cook the peaches in a grill pan on the stove top.) Then remove the peaches from the bowl and place them cut side down on the cooking grates. Reserve the remaining vinegar glaze.

3 Close the grill and cook for 5 minutes; then turn the peaches and grill them, uncovered, for 5 more minutes.

4 Place the grilled peaches on a serving platter and drizzle with the remaining glaze.

Edible Tips

♦ You can also slice the grilled peaches and serve them over a mixed field green and chicken salad for a light, tasty lunch.
♦ Peaches and ice cream make a great dessert. Cool the peaches for several minutes after grilling. Place the halves cut side up and top with a scoop of vanilla ice cream. Garnish with sprig of mint.

JAPANESE SWEET POTATO CASSEROLE

From Beverly Thomas, Cold Springs Farm, Weatherford

Here is the ultimate sweet potato dish, courtesy of Beverly Thomas of Cold Springs Farm in Weatherford. "Even if your family and friends say they absolutely hate sweet potato casserole, they'll declare their undying admiration for this one," says Thomas. She keeps the ingredients as light in color as possible to highlight the white color of the Japanese variety of sweet potatoes. Thomas grows many rare and heirloom vegetables, fruits, herbs, and flowers, and her CSA members are frequently treated to some interesting varieties. "I want that box to be like getting a present," says Thomas. "I want each family to be excited to open it every time they receive it." The Japanese sweet potato is the sweetest of all varieties, although you would never guess that by looking at the white color. It also has none of the stringiness common with the orange varieties, making it much smoother for casseroles or pies.

FOR THE CASSEROLE:
2 LB JAPANESE SWEET POTATOES, PEELED AND CUT INTO LARGE CUBES
1 STICK (8 TBSP) UNSALTED BUTTER, SOFTENED
1 CUP LIGHT-COLORED HONEY
½ CUP GRANULATED SUGAR, OR TO TASTE
2 TSP MEXICAN VANILLA EXTRACT
2 FARM-FRESH EGGS
½ CUP GOLDEN RAISINS

FOR THE TOPPING:
1½ CUPS PECAN HALVES
½ STICK (4 TBSP) UNSALTED BUTTER, MELTED
½ CUP FIRMLY PACKED LIGHT BROWN SUGAR

Serves 8

PREPARE THE CASSEROLE:

1 Preheat the oven to 350°F.

2 Place the sweet potatoes in a large pot of boiling water and cook until tender (you can also microwave them or roast them in the oven). Drain, and then place the potatoes in a large bowl and mash until smooth. Mix in the softened butter, honey, granulated sugar, and vanilla.

3 In a small bowl, whisk the eggs; fold them into the sweet potato mixture. Gently stir in the raisins. Pour the mixture into a 9 x 11-inch casserole dish and bake until firm, 20–30 minutes. Remove from the oven.

ADD THE TOPPING:

4 Cover the top of the casserole with the pecans. Drizzle half the melted butter over the pecans until covered. Sprinkle over the brown sugar; then drizzle with the remaining butter.

5 Return the casserole to the oven for 10 minutes; then turn on the broiler until the pecans are browned and the sugar has caramelized, about 5 minutes, but watch carefully so as to not let it burn. Serve warm.

OKRA IN BROWNED BUTTER

From Kim Pierce, freelance writer for the Dallas Morning News *and frequent contributor to* Edible Dallas & Fort Worth

Kim Pierce writes extensively about the North Texas locavore scene, but it was childhood visits to West Texas that opened her eyes to the goodness of garden-fresh produce. Her Hill Country German grandmother, who moved to West Texas as a young wife and mother, always kept a garden. She baked her own bread and made coffeecake, too. When the okra was ripe, she'd pick off enough spears for the noontime meal, carry them into the house in her apron, boil them, and coat the pods with browned salted butter. The nutty goodness of the butter brought out the best in these pods, which love the Texas heat.

1 LB SMALL TO MEDIUM OKRA PODS
½ STICK (4 TBSP) SALTED BUTTER
2 TBSP ALL-PURPOSE FLOUR
SALT
GRATED LEMON ZEST FOR GARNISH (OPTIONAL)

Serves 4

1 Rinse the okra pods and trim off the stem ends without breaking the pods. Put the okra in a steamer basket.

2 Add 1 cup water to a 4- to 5-quart pot big enough to hold the steamer basket. Bring the water to a boil over medium-high heat, insert the steamer basket, reduce the heat to a simmer, and cover, cooking the okra until it is just tender, 6–8 minutes. It's ready when a paring knife easily penetrates a pod but still meets a little resistance.

3 Remove the pot from the heat and carefully lift out the steamer basket. Pour off the water and return the pods to the pot. Cover and keep warm.

4 In a small skillet over medium-high heat, melt the butter. Add the flour and cook, stirring continuously, until the butter stops sizzling and you have a golden brown roux. Remove from the heat and continue stirring until the skillet cools slightly.

5 Add the browned butter roux to the okra, stirring gently to distribute over all the pods. Add salt to taste and garnish with lemon zest. Serve immediately.

QUINOA WITH OVEN-DRIED TEXAS TOMATOES, MUSHROOMS, ALMONDS, AND ASIAGO CHEESE

From Kim Pierce, freelance food writer for the Dallas Morning News *and frequent contributor to* Edible Dallas & Fort Worth

"In Texas, vine-ripened local tomatoes are something we eagerly await each year," says freelance food writer Kim Pierce, who's been touting regional food growers since the 1980s. "Some of my favorites come from farmer J.T. Lemley in Canton. He's been selling at the Dallas Farmers Market for at least as long as I've been writing." She suggests oven-drying some of your freshly picked tomatoes for a more intense flavor punch. Store a batch and savor the taste of summer long after the harvest. In this recipe, she uses Texas 1015 sweet onions, developed for the Texas climate and named for their planting date. This simple dish works year-round, and because quinoa is a complete protein, it makes a terrific vegetarian entrée. "If you can't get Asiago cheese," says Pierce, "be sure to substitute something robust, like Parmesan, because the cheese makes the dish."

Edible Tips

♦ Most boxed quinoa has been prerinsed, but give it a quick rinse anyway to remove any trace of saponin, a bitter-tasting coating found on the plant in its natural state.

♦ Any type of quinoa (red or white) will work with this recipe. Cooking times may vary depending on the type.

1¼ CUPS WATER OR LOW-SODIUM CHICKEN BROTH
1 CUP RED OR WHITE QUINOA, RINSED AND DRAINED
½ CUP SLIVERED BLANCHED ALMONDS
1 TBSP OLIVE OIL
1 MEDIUM ONION, DICED (ABOUT ¾ CUP)
1 LB MUSHROOMS, PREFERABLY SHIITAKES, STEMS REMOVED AND SLICED
½ CUP OVEN-DRIED TOMATOES (RECIPE ON PAGE 84), ROUGH DICED
SALT
½ CUP SHREDDED ASIAGO CHEESE

Serves 4

1 Heat the water to boiling over medium-high heat, stir in the quinoa, and reduce the heat to a simmer. Cook, uncovered, about 15 minutes or according to package directions. Remove from the heat; set aside.

2 In a large dry skillet over medium-high heat, toast the almonds, shaking the pan or stirring, until they are lightly browned and fragrant. Move the almonds to a small bowl.

3 Return the skillet to medium heat and add the olive oil. Add the onion and cook, stirring occasionally, until translucent and caramelized, about 5 minutes. Move the onion to the edge of the skillet and add the mushrooms. Cook, stirring occasionally, until the mushrooms begin to brown and release their moisture. Then reduce the heat under the skillet to low.

4 Fluff the quinoa with a fork and add to the skillet mixture along with the oven-dried tomatoes, stirring gently to combine. Season with salt to taste. (Remember, the cheese that you will be adding is salty, so don't overdo it.)

5 Add half the cheese to the skillet and blend well to combine. Remove from the heat, sprinkle the remaining cheese on top, and serve.

OVEN-DRIED TOMATOES

From Kim Pierce, freelance food writer for the Dallas Morning News *and frequent contributor to* Edible Dallas & Fort Worth

These homemade dried tomatoes are great on pizzas, added to pasta, or enjoyed as a snack.

4–5 CUPS CHERRY TOMATOES

1 TSP SALT

Makes about 2 cups

1 Preheat the oven to its lowest setting, 175°F or 200°F. Line 2 baking sheets with parchment paper or silicone baking mats.

2 Rinse the tomatoes and pat dry. Slice in half lengthwise.

3 Place the tomatoes, cut side up, about 1 inch apart on the prepared baking sheets. Sprinkle with the salt. Leave in the oven 6–12 hours, checking every so often. When done, the tomatoes will be flexible but not brittle.

4 Cool the dried tomatoes completely; then store in zip-top plastic bags in the refrigerator or freezer.

SMOKY GLAZED VEGETABLES

From André Natera,
Pyramid Restaurant and Bar at
the Fairmont Dallas

In the huddle of Dallas's sleek down-town skyscrapers, there's a tranquil three-thousand-square-foot terrace garden tended by a chef who draws his inspira-tion from Mother Nature. She's "the true workhorse in the kitchen," says André Natera, executive chef of the venera-ble Pyramid Restaurant at the Fairmont Dallas hotel. Natera takes a fresh-market approach to cooking. "I believe in keeping things uncomplicated and giving respect to nature. If it grows together, it probably goes together." Here, he adds a tablespoon of Texas Olive Ranch's Mesquite-Smoked Olive Oil to infuse this spring medley with the hinted flavors of a woodsy campfire.

4 MEDIUM FRESH MOREL
    MUSHROOMS, RINSED, PATTED
    DRY, AND CUT INTO ½-INCH
    PIECES
4 FINGERLING POTATOES, CUT INTO
    ½-INCH PIECES
8 BABY CARROTS
1 DRIED BAY LEAF
LEAVES FROM 1 SPRIG FRESH
    THYME, CHOPPED
1 TBSP SMOKED OLIVE OIL, TEXAS
    OLIVE RANCH MESQUITE-SMOKED
    PREFERRED

1½–2 CUPS CHICKEN STOCK
12 THICK ASPARAGUS SPEARS,
    BOTTOMS TRIMMED AND SPEARS
    CUT INTO 2-INCH PIECES
    ON THE DIAGONAL
8 CHERRY TOMATOES
SALT
FRESHLY GROUND BLACK PEPPER
2 TBSP CHOPPED FRESH PARSLEY

Serves 4

1 Combine the mushrooms, potatoes, carrots, bay leaf, thyme, olive oil, and 1 cup of the stock in a saucepan big enough to hold them without overcrowding. Cook over high heat until almost all the liquid has evaporated, about 15 minutes.

2 Add the asparagus and tomatoes and ½ cup of the stock. Continue cooking over medium high heat until the liquid is reduced to a glaze, about 20 minutes. If the potatoes and carrots need more cooking time, add the remaining ½ cup stock and cook until this liquid has also been reduced to a glaze.

3 Season to taste with salt and pepper and sprinkle with the parsley.

A MOTLEY WILTED CHARD AND ARUGULA POTATO SALAD

*From Tom and Becca Motley,
Tom Motley North Texas Gardens,
McKinney*

Long popular in Italy and France, the peppery green leaves of arugula, or rocket as it's called in France, have finally made a name for themselves in North Texas. Organic gardeners Tom and Becca Motley grow herbs and produce at various locations around Collin County for their McKinney neighbors at Café Málaga, Square Burger, and Local Yocal. Perhaps because they're also painters, they chose Rainbow Swiss chard with its unique, colorful stalks and large crinkled leaves to match with their spicy arugula. Garlic, olive oil, and roasted potatoes provide even more layers of flavor in this simple but savory dish. Gardener Motley suggests serving crumbles of earthy Gorgonzola and a crunchy French baguette on the side.

20 SMALL YUKON GOLD OR NEW
  POTATOES, DICED (NOT PEELED)
⅔ CUP BEST-QUALITY OLIVE OIL
KOSHER SALT
FRESHLY GROUND BLACK PEPPER
30 LARGE LEAVES RAINBOW SWISS
  CHARD
1 SMALL ONION, DICED

2 CLOVES GARLIC, DICED
1 CUP ARUGULA, TORN INTO LARGE
  PIECES
CRUMBLED GORGONZOLA CHEESE
  FOR GARNISH (OPTIONAL)
FRENCH BREAD FOR SERVING

Serves 10

1 Put an oven rack in the middle of the oven and preheat the broiler. In a large roasting pan, toss the potatoes with ¼ cup of the olive oil, turning them several times to coat well with the oil. Season lightly with salt and pepper, and low-broil the potatoes on the middle rack for 8–10 minutes on one side; then turn the potatoes and return to the broiler for another 8–10 minutes. Remove from the oven; set aside.

2 Prepare the chard by removing their thick center stems. Chop the stems into ½-inch pieces and set them aside. Tear the leaves into thirds and set them aside separately from the stems.

3 Place a covered wok or large skillet over medium heat and add the remaining olive oil. When it shimmers, sauté the onion, garlic, and chopped chard stems until the onion begins to turn translucent and the chard stems soften, about 5 minutes. Fold in the roasted potatoes. Top with the chard leaves and arugula and cover. Reduce the heat to low and sweat the vegetables together for 2 minutes.

4 Remove from the burner and let the contents rest for 5 minutes before serving. Serve with crumbled Gorgonzola if you like and crunchy French bread on side.

SMOKIN' BEANS IN THREE COLORS

*From Jim Henry and
Karen Lee Henry, Texas Olive Ranch*

There's a new kind of oil business booming in Texas, and this liquid gold is of an edible type. Since 1994, Jim Henry at the Texas Olive Ranch has been at the forefront of this burgeoning industry. His ranch is located near Carrizo Springs, halfway between San Antonio and the Mexican border. The terrain is flat, with a sandy loam soil similar to that in the southern parts of Spain, where olive orchards have flourished for centuries. The Texas Olive Ranch has more than forty thousand olive trees, including two Spanish varieties (Arbequina and Arbosana) and a Greek variety (Koroneiki). Olive oil so permeates traditional Mediterranean cultures that even the campesinos working in the fields use it as a dressing for their simple noonday meals.

Like the Texas border, this three-bean dish draws on several cultural traditions: cannellini beans, a favorite in Italian cuisine; red beans, from the kitchens of New Orleans; and black beans, a staple in Latin American cuisine.

1 CUP DRIED WHITE CANNELLINI BEANS

1 CUP DRIED SMALL RED BEANS (SOMETIMES CALLED LOUISIANA RED BEANS OR MEXICAN RED BEANS)

1 CUP DRIED BLACK BEANS

½ CUP SMOKED OLIVE OIL, TEXAS OLIVE RANCH MESQUITE-SMOKED PREFERRED

JUICE OF 1 LIME OR LEMON

½ CUP COARSELY CHOPPED FRESH CILANTRO

4 LARGE HEIRLOOM TOMATOES, CHOPPED (ABOUT 2 CUPS)

1 JALAPEÑO CHILE, DICED (INCLUDE SEEDS IF EXTRA HEAT IS DESIRED) (OPTIONAL)

SEA SALT

FRESHLY GROUND BLACK PEPPER

½ CUP CRUMBLED QUESO FRESCO FOR GARNISH (OPTIONAL)

FRESH CORN TORTILLAS

Serves about 12

1 Rinse each bean variety separately, place in separate 5-quart cooking pots, cover each with 2 inches of water, and allow to soak overnight.

2 Drain the beans separately and refill each pot with about 2 quarts of water. Return the beans to their pots and bring each to a boil over medium-high heat. Once the water is boiling, reduce the heat to low and simmer until all the beans are tender but still firm, 45–60 minutes for the cannellini, and 1–1½ hours for the small red beans and black beans.

3 Drain; then gently combine the cooked beans in a large serving bowl. Drizzle with the olive oil and lime or lemon juice and stir gently to mix. Toss in the cilantro, tomatoes, and jalapeño, if desired. Season with salt and pepper to taste and garnish with crumbled queso fresco, if desired. Serve immediately, with plenty of fresh corn tortillas.

SWISS CHARD LASAGNA

From Linn Madsen, Savoy Sorbet, Dallas

Selling her herb-infused Savoy Sorbet at farmers' markets for the past three years has taught Linn Madsen the value of "locally, lovingly, hopefully organically grown food." She confesses that Swiss chard, a fairly recent addition to North Texas markets, was new to her, and she decided to make lasagna with it, substituting chard for the noodles. "The grand experiment worked," she says, "and I'll probably never use lasagna noodles again." She likes the hydroponically grown chard that's become popular with local producers, such as Elliott Grows, based in Argyle. They bring fresh greens to the markets year-round.

Edible Tip

This is an elastic recipe; you can adjust to your taste, as well as add sausage, or any number of extra veggies, such as thin-sliced peppers, onions, and zucchini.

1 (32 OZ) CONTAINER RICOTTA CHEESE
1 CUP FRESHLY GRATED PARMESAN CHEESE
1 LARGE EGG
3 CLOVES GARLIC, MINCED
2 TBSP CHOPPED FRESH BASIL OR 2 HEAPING TSP DRIED
SALT
FRESHLY GROUND BLACK PEPPER
2 CUPS HOMEMADE MARINARA SAUCE (PAGE 108)
12–15 LARGE LEAVES SWISS CHARD, STEMS REMOVED
1 CUP SHREDDED MOZZARELLA CHEESE

Serves 4–6

1 Preheat the oven to 350°F. Lightly grease a 15 x 10-inch casserole dish.

2 In a large bowl, mix together the ricotta, ½ cup of the Parmesan, and the egg, garlic, and basil. Season to taste with salt and pepper.

3 Spread about ½ cup marinara sauce around the bottom of the prepared dish. Place 5 chard leaves on top of the sauce. Spoon one-third of the ricotta mixture over the chard leaves and, with the back of a spoon, spread to cover. Sprinkle ⅓ cup of the mozzarella on top of the ricotta mixture. Repeat the process twice more, ending with the marinara. Sprinkle the top with the remaining ½ cup Parmesan.

4 Bake the lasagna until it's nicely bubbly and slightly browned, 30–40 minutes. Remove from the oven and let rest 10 minutes before serving.

ROASTED SWEET POTATO RAVIOLI WITH SAGE AND HAZELNUT BROWN BUTTER

From Katy Lopez, chef contributor to
Edible Dallas & Fort Worth

East Texas is home to some of the nation's finest sweet potatoes. In the Piney Woods town of Gilmer, there's an annual "Yamboree" festival celebrating this orange-hued root vegetable—even if the belle of the ball is officially a sweet potato. Since the 1930s we've been using the terms interchangeably, and it's a tough habit to change. No matter what you call them, they're an outstanding source of beta-carotene and vitamin A, and they're delicious. This recipe for sweet potato ravioli with a luscious hazelnut sauce makes a great winter side dish. The wonton wrappers are a time-saver and really let the caramelized flavor in the filling stand out.

Edible Tip

Don't substitute dried sage for fresh in this recipe. Its flavor is the key.

FOR THE RAVIOLI:

4 LARGE SWEET POTATOES, PEELED AND CUT INTO 1½-INCH CUBES (ABOUT 3½ CUPS)
2 TBSP OLIVE OIL
2 TSP SALT
3 TBSP FIRMLY PACKED LIGHT BROWN SUGAR
½ TSP GROUND NUTMEG
½ CUP MASCARPONE CHEESE
1 TSP GROUND CINNAMON
60 WONTON WRAPPERS
2 LARGE EGG WHITES, BEATEN

FOR THE SAUCE:

2 STICKS (16 TBSP) BUTTER
¼ CUP COARSELY GROUND HAZELNUTS
¼ CUP HEAVY CREAM
2 TBSP CHOPPED FRESH SAGE
¼ TSP GROUND NUTMEG
SALT
FRESHLY GROUND BLACK PEPPER

Serves 6

MAKE THE RAVIOLI:

1 Preheat the oven to 425°F. Line a baking sheet with parchment paper. Toss the sweet potato cubes with the olive oil, salt, and 1 tablespoon of the brown sugar. Pour the cubes onto the prepared baking sheet, arrange in a single layer, and bake until tender, 35–40 minutes.

2 Let the sweet potatoes cool slightly: then transfer them to a food processor. Add the remaining 2 tablespoons brown sugar, the nutmeg, mascarpone, and cinnamon, and pulse until smooth.

3 Place 3 wonton wrappers on a lightly floured work surface. Use a pastry brush to brush the edges of each wrapper with the egg whites. Place 1 tablespoon sweet potato filling in the center of each wrapper. Top each one with a wrapper and press the edges together to seal. Transfer ravioli to a clean parchment paper–lined baking sheet and cover the sheet with plastic wrap. Make and cover remaining ravioli in same manner. Chill for up to 3 hours.

MAKE THE SAUCE:

4 Melt the butter in a medium sauté pan over medium-high heat. Add the ground hazelnuts and sauté until golden brown, 3–4 minutes. Stir in the cream and cook for 1 minute. Add the sage and nutmeg. Season with salt and pepper to taste. Keep warm.

5 Meanwhile, bring a large pot of water to boil over high heat. Drop the ravioli in the pot and cook until just tender, about 2 minutes. Drain the ravioli and serve with the butter sauce drizzled over them.

CHAPTER 4

MAINS

Texas is cattle country, and our state's colorful
ranching history is reflected in these pages. There's a recipe for our beloved
chicken-fried steak and another for saucy beef short ribs. And what Lone
Star State cookbook is complete without chili con carne? As Gulf State resi-
dents, we have a passion for shrimp and fish. We love our local fishmongers
and those intrepid seafood purveyors who set up at farmers' markets and
roadside stands bearing ice chests from the coast. During hunting season,
there's venison and quail. Chicken and pork? We love them too. We're a car-
nivorous state, but we appreciate our vegetables with equal fervor. Though
only one vegetarian entrée is listed in this chapter, many of our side dishes
would make hearty meat-free meals.

CHICKEN ROULADES WITH
GOAT CHEESE AND SPINACH

From Katy Lopez, chef contributor to
Edible Dallas & Fort Worth

The French know a thing or two about giving chicken breasts plenty of richness and flavor—and not coincidentally, it was in Paris that Deborah Rogers, then working as a model for the Eileen Ford Agency, learned the basics of traditional French cheese making. She returned to Texas and was disappointed to find that no one was selling the soft goat's milk chèvre that she'd come to love. So what was a girl to do? How about buying two goats—Freckles and Bea—and making it yourself? Today Deborah has fifty milkers and Deborah's Farmstead Cheese is featured in some of our best restaurants. Our contributor Katy Lopez loads Deborah's cheese into these roulades for a simple (but quite elegant) dish.

Edible Tip

These can be made a day ahead of time and stored in the refrigerator, but wait to brush with butter until you are ready to bake them.

2 WHOLE SKINLESS BONELESS
PASTURE-RAISED CHICKEN
BREASTS (ABOUT 8 OZ EACH)
2 TBSP OLIVE OIL
3 CLOVES GARLIC, MINCED
¼ CUP CHOPPED SHALLOTS
8 OZ GOAT CHEESE
2 OZ CREAM CHEESE, SOFTENED
8 OZ FRESH BABY SPINACH

3 TBSP UNSALTED BUTTER, MELTED
SALT
FRESHLY GROUND BLACK PEPPER

SPECIAL EQUIPMENT:
BUTCHER'S STRING AND
TOOTHPICKS

Serves 4

1 Preheat the oven to 350°F. Line a baking sheet with parchment paper.

2 Pat the chicken dry and pound it to a ⅜-inch thickness, one piece at a time, between two sheets of plastic wrap. Return the chicken to the fridge, covered, while you prepare the filling.

3 In a medium skillet over medium heat, heat the olive oil; then sauté the garlic and shallots until tender, about 2 minutes. Remove from the heat and let cool for several minutes.

4 In a medium bowl, blend together the goat cheese and cream cheese with an electric mixer. Add the garlic and shallots and blend well.

5 Fill a large pot with water and bring to a boil. Blanch the spinach for 30 seconds; then remove, drain, and plunge into a bowl of ice water to stop the cooking and set the color. Drain again and remove excess water from the spinach by gently squeezing it.

6 On each piece of chicken, spread one-fourth of the goat cheese mixture evenly; be careful not to go all the way to the edges. On top of the cheese mixture, spread a generous layer of blanched spinach. Roll the chicken to enclose the filling, tie with butcher's string, and secure the edge with a toothpick. Brush with the melted butter and generously season the outside of the chicken with salt and pepper.

7 Place the chicken roulades on the prepared baking sheet and bake until the temperature in the center of each reaches 165°F on an instant-read thermometer, about 35 minutes. Turn the oven to broil and place the chicken on the top rack of the oven for 3 minutes to create a crust.

8 Slice the roulades into rounds and serve as an entrée or slice on a bias and serve over pasta, such as linguine, with a basic lemon-butter sauce.

MAINS

CRISPY CHICKEN WITH BLUE GRITS

From Robert Lyford, Patina Green Home and Market, McKinney

"Work with the very best ingredients and then don't mess 'em up!" So goes the cooking philosophy of chef Robert Lyford of Patina Green Home and Market in historic downtown McKinney. "That's especially important for recipes with only a few ingredients," says Lyford. "Like my Crispy Chicken with Blue Grits. This is *not* the recipe for supermarket chicken and boxed grits." Lyford uses pasture-raised chicken from Windy Meadows Family Farm. "They have exceptional flavor. I prefer the boneless thighs instead of the breasts, because they're always juicy and tender." And he loves the locally milled blue corn grits he buys from Homestead Gristmill in Waco. "They are coarse ground but are smooth and creamy when finished. The cheese I use is Brazos Valley Blueberry Havarti, also made at Homestead Farms. The flecks of blueberries add a nice bit of color to the grits, but any blue cheese will work well here too. Just use the best and freshest local ingredients you can find."

2½ TSP SALT

1 CUP BLUE CORN GRITS

1 LB SKIN-ON BONELESS CHICKEN
    THIGHS (6 THIGHS)

8 OZ BLUEBERRY HAVARTI OR
    BLUE CHEESE, GRATED

Serves 6

1 In a 3-quart saucepan, bring 4 cups water to a boil and add 2 teaspoons of the salt. Whisk in the grits, reduce the heat to low, and cover. Simmer until the grits are creamy, about 30 minutes, whisking frequently to prevent sticking. If the grits begin to thicken and look a little dry, add 1–2 tablespoons water. When they are completely cooked and tender, remove from the heat and let rest for 5 minutes.

2 When the grits are about half cooked, preheat a large, heavy skillet (preferably cast iron) over medium-high heat. While the pan preheats, season the chicken thighs generously with the remaining ½ teaspoon salt. Place the thighs skin side down in the hot pan and cook without moving the pieces until the skin is crispy and golden brown, 4–5 minutes. Turn the pieces over, reduce the heat to medium, and cook until the meat is cooked through, another 3–5 minutes. Remove the chicken from the pan to a platter and let rest 5 minutes.

3 When ready to serve, whisk any chicken jus that has collected on the platter into the grits; then stir in the cheese. Serve a dollop of grits with each piece of crispy chicken.

TEXAS CHICKEN-FRIED STEAK AND CREAM GRAVY

From Heather Hamilton, Genesis Beef and Local Yocal Farm to Market, McKinney

Matt Hamilton's family has been in ranching since 1905, and he and his dad started raising grass-fed beef in 2008. In an effort to control the processing step, Matt and his wife, Heather, bought a building in historic downtown McKinney in 2010. Later that year, they opened their butcher shop, Local Yocal, where they sell their beef and local artisanal foods, from organic cheese to cookies and sustainably grown produce. Around the corner, Square Burgers serves their beef exclusively.

Edible Tips

• If all of your steaks do not fit in the skillet at once, you'll probably need to add more oil between batches.

• If you want to make more gravy, just add milk and flour proportionately: The perfect ratio is 1 cup milk to 1 heaping tablespoon flour. Mixing the flour and milk together before cooking, rather than whisking the milk and flour in the hot skillet, produces the most consistent, lump-free gravy for a novice gravy maker.

1½ LB GRASS-FED ROUND STEAK, POUNDED TO A ¾-INCH THICKNESS
1½ CUPS PLUS 1 TBSP FLOUR
KOSHER SALT
FRESHLY GROUND BLACK PEPPER
3 EGGS
1¾ CUPS WHOLE MILK OR HALF-AND-HALF
¾ CUP CANOLA OR GRAPESEED OIL, FOR FRYING
1 TBSP BUTTER

Serves 4

1 Lay the round steak flat and pat dry with paper towels. Cut into 4 equal portions; set aside.

2 Prepare 2 pie plates with contents for battering. In one, combine 1½ cups of the flour with salt and pepper to taste. In the other, whisk the eggs and ¾ cup of the milk together until completely blended.

3 Heat a 10- to 12-inch cast-iron skillet over medium-high heat and add the oil. The oil should be no more than ¼ inch deep—just enough to come up about a third of the way on the steaks.

4 While the skillet and oil are heating, begin battering the steaks. Dip both sides of the steaks into the flour mixture first; then transfer to the egg-milk mixture to lightly coat both sides with the liquid. Repeat these steps one more time.

5 Test that the oil is hot enough by tossing a pinch of flour into the pan. If it immediately sizzles, the oil is ready. Use tongs to gently place the steaks in the oil, being careful not to splatter oil or overcrowd the meat. Cook the steaks about 5 minutes, until the bottoms are golden brown. Carefully flip and cook for another 5 minutes. Press on the steak with a fork. If the juice runs mostly clear, the steak is done. Transfer the steaks to a paper towel–lined platter and keep warm.

6 Once the steaks are done, combine the remaining 1 tablespoon flour and the remaining 1 cup milk in a small bowl. Whisk to blend. Melt the butter in the skillet with the steak drippings. Add the milk-flour mixture to the skillet and stir, scraping up all the browned bits from the bottom of the skillet. Continue cooking and stirring until the mixture thickens. If it boils, reduce the heat to medium. Season the gravy with salt and pepper to taste.

7 Plate the steaks with the gravy on top, or pass the steaks on a platter and the gravy in a bowl.

MAINS

97

ORANGE SRIRACHA-GLAZED CHICKEN WITH ANCHO-CITRUS RELISH

*From Cosme Alcantar,
Blue Mesa Grill, five locations in the
Dallas & Fort Worth Metroplex*

The Southwest meets the Far East in this citrus-rich dish from executive chef Cosme Alcantar. Blue Mesa Grill owners Jim and Liz Baron strive to utilize seasonal ingredients, and in the chilly middle of the Texas winter, a fresh harvest of citrus—navel oranges, Meyer lemons, and ruby-colored grapefruit—arrives from the Rio Grande Valley, adding spark and sparkle to their restaurant's menu. In this recipe, the chicken is brined to add moisture and flavor and then glazed with a coating of sriracha sauce and orange marmalade. Each grilled breast is topped with a chunky relish of sweet oranges flavored with smoky ancho chili powder. Serve with Blue Mesa's Asparagus Gremolata with Ginger Rice (page 68).

FOR BRINING THE CHICKEN:

½ CUP KOSHER SALT OR ¼ CUP TABLE SALT

½ CUP SUGAR

4 (6 OZ) SKINLESS, BONELESS CHICKEN BREASTS

FOR THE RELISH:

JUICE OF 2 LIMES

2 TBSP OLIVE OIL

½ TSP ANCHO CHILI POWDER

8 ORANGE SEGMENTS, WHITE PITH REMOVED, ROUGHLY CHOPPED

3 SCALLIONS (WHITE PARTS AND SOME OF THE GREEN), THINLY SLICED

3 TBSP CHOPPED FRESH MINT

FOR THE GLAZE:

1 CUP ORANGE MARMALADE

2 TBSP SOY SAUCE

1 TBSP TOASTED SESAME OIL

1 TBSP RICE WINE VINEGAR

1 TBSP SRIRACHA SAUCE

TO FINISH THE DISH:

¼ TSP FRESHLY GROUND BLACK PEPPER

½ TSP SALT

Serves 4

BRINE THE CHICKEN:

1 Fill a large container with 4 quarts water. Pour the salt and sugar into the water and stir until dissolved. Put the chicken breasts in the brine, cover, and refrigerate for 1½–2 hours.

MAKE THE RELISH:

2 In a medium bowl, combine the lime juice, olive oil, chili powder, chopped orange, scallions, and mint until the pieces of orange are evenly coated with juice, oil, and seasonings. Cover and refrigerate.

MAKE THE GLAZE:

3 Combine the marmalade, soy sauce, sesame oil, vinegar, and sriracha sauce to a rolling boil and continue to cook on high heat for 3 minutes. Remove from the heat and cool before using to baste the chicken.

FINISH THE DISH:

4 Preheat the grill (or a grill pan) to medium-high. Remove the chicken from the brine and dry with a paper towel. Season with the salt and pepper; then grill until an instant-read thermometer inserted into the thickest part of each reads 165°F, 5–7 minutes per side. Brush with the glaze 5 minutes before the chicken is done. Glaze again on other side about a minute before removing from the grill.

5 To serve, top each grilled breast with one-quarter of the relish.

MAINS

BEEF GYRO MEATBALLS WITH ROASTED EGGPLANT SALAD AND GREEK YOGURT

From Dena Peterson, Café Modern, Modern Art Museum of Fort Worth

Café Modern, the sleek eatery at the Modern Art Museum of Fort Worth, shares its soaring glass walls with Rothko, Pollock, Warhol, and Picasso. Here chef Dena Peterson creates dishes inspired by both artists and farmers as well as the changing of the seasons. She makes weekly treks to the Cowtown Farmers Market, where most of the ingredients in this recipe can be found from the late spring through the summer. The restaurant's onions, tomatoes, and eggplants are grown at Scott Farms in Rising Star. Another resource for vegetables and herbs is B & G's Garden in Poolville. For olive oil, Peterson depends on Jim Henry at the Texas Olive Ranch in Carrizo Springs. The restaurant's resource for juicy and flavorful Wagyu beef is the Strube Ranch in Pittsburg. This dish features a Wagyu beef version of Greek meatballs atop a salad of roasted eggplant and fresh tomatoes.

FOR THE SALAD:
2 LARGE EGGPLANTS
1 SMALL RED ONION, MINCED
2 CLOVES GARLIC, MINCED
2 LARGE TOMATOES, PEELED, SEEDED, AND DICED
¼ CUP OLIVE OIL (TEXAS OLIVE RANCH ARBEQUINA PREFERRED)
JUICE OF 1 LEMON
SALT
FRESHLY GROUND BLACK PEPPER
¼ CUP FINELY CHOPPED FRESH FLAT-LEAF PARSLEY

FOR THE MEATBALLS:
2½ LB GROUND BEEF (STRUBE RANCH WAGYU PREFERRED)
1 MEDIUM ONION, VERY FINELY CHOPPED
1½ CUPS FRESH WHITE BREADCRUMBS (6 SLICES, CRUSTS REMOVED AND CRUMBLED)
1 TBSP FINELY MINCED GARLIC
1 TBSP CHOPPED FRESH MARJORAM
1 TBSP CHOPPED FRESH ROSEMARY
2 TBSP CHOPPED FRESH FLAT-LEAF PARSLEY
¼ TSP GROUND NUTMEG
1 TBSP KOSHER SALT
½ TSP FRESHLY GROUND BLACK PEPPER
1 LARGE EGG, BEATEN

FOR SERVING:
1 CUP PLAIN GREEK YOGURT
OLIVE OIL (TEXAS OLIVE RANCH PREFERRED)
3 TBSP PINE NUTS, TOASTED

Serves 6

MAKE THE SALAD:

1 Preheat the oven to 375°F. Place the whole eggplants on a baking sheet and roast until they collapse and are completely soft, 1–1½ hours. Remove from the oven, but leave the oven on. Carefully cut the eggplants in half to release the steam. Let cool completely; then peel off and discard the skins.

2 Place the eggplant pulp in a large bowl. Stir in the onion, garlic, and tomatoes with a silicone spatula. Drizzle with the olive oil and lemon juice, and mix to combine. Season to taste with salt and pepper and garnish with the parsley. Cover and keep chilled until ready to serve.

MAKE THE MEATBALLS:

3 Place the beef, onion, breadcrumbs, garlic, herbs, nutmeg, salt, pepper, egg, and ¼ cup water in a large bowl. Using clean hands, thoroughly combine the ingredients. Form the mixture into 2-inch meatballs. You will have 18–20 meatballs.

Edible Tips

- Roast the eggplant while you are prepping the meatballs, or even the day before to save time.
- For a smokier flavor, roast the eggplant over medium-high heat on a grill.

4 Lightly coat a sheet pan with cooking spray, place the meatballs on it a few inches apart, and roast them until cooked through, 20–25 minutes.

ASSEMBLE THE DISH:

5 To serve, place 3 meatballs, about ½ cup eggplant salad, and 2 tablespoons yogurt on each plate. Drizzle with a bit of olive oil and sprinkle with the toasted pine nuts.

QUAIL BREASTS WITH BACON, JALAPEÑO, AND CHEESE STUFFING

From Chris Hughes, Broken Arrow Ranch, Ingram and Diamond H Ranch, Bandera

Quail has long been a popular game bird in Texas. Its delicately flavored meat has a unique taste, somewhat akin to the dark meat of a free-range chicken. The sport of quail hunting is a Texas tradition, but in recent years, the native quail populations have been steadily declining, not only in the Southwest but all across the United States. Loss of the native grasses that are a covey's natural habitat is one of many factors being investigated. At Diamond H Ranch in Bandera, the quail are being raised for both field and table on an all-natural diet. This recipe for stuffed quail is a riff on the Texas hunter's campfire tradition of combining quail with jalapeño and wrapping it with a slice of bacon. Chris Hughes of Broken Arrow and Diamond H ranches has concocted this version with a yummy cheddar cheese stuffing that has a peppery kick.

Edible Tip

Diamond H Ranch in Bandera sells farm-raised boneless quail breasts. You can visit the ranch yourself, or purchase online at DiamondHQuail.com.

4 CUPS 1-INCH BREAD CUBES
6 SLICES BACON, CUT INTO SMALL PIECES
½ TSP MINCED GARLIC
½ CUP CHOPPED ONION
2–3 JALAPEÑO CHILES, SEEDED AND CHOPPED
¾–1 CUP CHICKEN BROTH
1 CUP GRATED CHEDDAR CHEESE
SALT
FRESHLY GROUND BLACK PEPPER
8 BONELESS QUAIL BREASTS
OLIVE OIL
CHILI POWDER

Serves 4

1 Preheat the oven to 400°F. Spread the bread cubes on a baking sheet and toast until they're a rich golden brown, 5–10 minutes.

2 Cook the bacon in a large pan over medium-high heat until it is just starting to turn golden but not yet crisp, 5–6 minutes, stirring a few times. Drain the fat from the pan until about 2 tablespoons remain.

3 Return the pan to the heat and add the garlic, onion, and jalapeños. Sauté for 5 minutes, until the onion is translucent and the jalapeños are soft. Deglaze the pan with ¼ cup of the broth. Add the toasted bread cubes. Gently mix the stuffing and add more broth ¼ cup at a time, until the bread is moist but not soggy. Stir in the grated cheese. Remove the pan from the heat and let the stuffing cool. Season to taste with salt and pepper.

4 Pat the quail breasts dry with a paper towel. Gently loosen the skin from the breast meat, leaving it attached on the sides, and stuff the pocket generously with the stuffing. If the skin pulls free, you can secure the stuffing by using grill-safe metal or wooden skewers. Rub the skins with olive oil, and season lightly with salt, pepper, and chili powder.

5 Heat the grill to medium. Begin grilling the breasts with the skin side up, and cook for 5–7 minutes. Use tongs to flip the breasts and cook another 5 minutes. Quail meat is done when it feels firm to the touch.

CEVOLA FAMILY EGGPLANT PARMIGIANA

*From Alfonso Cevola,
hoja santa grower for The Mozzarella
Company, Dallas*

A wine professional by trade, Alfonso Cevola is one of a handful of hoja santa growers for Paula Lambert's Mozzarella Company. The huge leaves are used to wrap her prizewinning Hoja Santa Goat Cheese, imparting a wonderful, herby flavor. When it's time to make this Calabrian family recipe, Cevola uses Paula's fresh mozzarella as part of the cheese mix. This dish is not like any eggplant Parmesan you've ever tasted. It's more in the tradition of a timpano. Cevola has given it a Texas twist by grilling the eggplant slices rather than roasting them, making the dish more rustic and complex.

Edible Tips

• Don't worry if some of the eggplant slices get too dark on the grill; you can still use them. The main thing is to cook the eggplant so it isn't tough. As you cook the eggplant, the skins will soften up, too.
• This is a fairly free-form casserole and often winds up making 1 large casserole for immediate eating and 1 small one that you can freeze and heat up later.

4–5 MEDIUM EGGPLANTS
SALT
OLIVE OIL AS NEEDED FOR
  GRILLING
8–9 HARD-COOKED EGGS
2 (8 OZ) BALLS FRESH MOZZARELLA
  CHEESE
1 (25.5 OZ) JAR MUIR GLEN
  CABERNET MARINARA SAUCE OR
  OTHER MARINARA SAUCE

2 CUPS GRATED WHOLE-MILK
  MOZZARELLA CHEESE
1 CUP SHREDDED PARMESAN
  CHEESE

Serves 8

1 Place one baking rack on each of several baking racks on top of a baking sheet. Slice the eggplant into ¼-inch-thick medallions and place the slices on the racks. Let drain for 30 minutes, and then pat the slices dry with paper towels. Sprinkle the slices with salt and drizzle with olive oil, and then flip the slices and sprinkle again with salt and oil.

2 Preheat the grill to medium-high (375°F on a gas grill). Grill the eggplant until golden (they should have visible grill marks), about 5 minutes. Flip the slices and grill the other side. Remove from the grill and keep warm.

3 Using an egg slicer, cut the eggs into horizontal medallions. Set aside.

4 Pull or slice the fresh mozzarella balls into small pieces, about as big as your thumb. Set aside. Preheat the oven to 350°F.

5 Select a 1½- to 2-quart ovenproof glass or stoneware casserole dish for your eggplant Parmigiana. Do not use metal, as it may react with the marinara sauce and create an off flavor in the dish. (You may need 2 casseroles, depending on their size.) Coat the dish lightly with olive oil. Spread a thin layer of marinara sauce on the bottom. Add a layer of eggplant, covering the sauce. Dot with some egg slices and a few pieces of fresh mozzarella, and fill in the spaces with the mozzarella. Add a thin layer of Parmesan. Repeat the process, ending with the marinara sauce and a light sprinkling of grated mozzarella. Bake, uncovered, for 35–45 minutes, until bubbly.

6 To serve, cut into slices like you would a layer cake, so every slice has visible layers.

SPICY DRY STEAM-SMOKED
PORK BELLY RIBS

From Elissa Altman,
Edible Communities, Inc.

If baby back ribs are the petite dainties of the barbecue world, then these smoky pork belly ribs are the big daddies: dense, juicy, and fall-apart tender, they're what happens when you leave bacon on the bone, massage it with an eye-tearingly spicy dry rub, and then slow smoke it until all its gorgeous fat melts into thick ribbons of pork meat and it hollers *Texas* at the top of its lungs. It may take a little time, but once they're done, you'll have mammoth, lip-smackin' smoked pork ribs that will have you saying "Adios, amigo" to any other wussy-man kind. Serve these big boys with a sweet barbecue sauce to offset the heat of the rub, pass around ice-cold beers, put Lefty Frizzell on the record player, and remember the good ol' days when cowboys were king and even vegetarians bent their rules for some great barbecue.

FOR THE DRY RUB:
¼ CUP TURBINADO SUGAR
2 TBSP DRY MUSTARD
½ CUP SWEET PIMENTÓN
¼ CUP GARLIC POWDER
¼ CUP FINELY GROUND SEA SALT
¼ CUP CUMIN SEEDS, TOASTED AND GROUND
1 TBSP GROUND SZECHUAN PEPPERCORNS
1 TBSP FINELY GROUND BLACK PEPPER
¼ CUP ANCHO CHILI POWDER
2 TBSP CAYENNE

FOR THE RIBS:
8 PORK BELLY RIBS

SPECIAL TOOLS:
HICKORY WOOD CHIPS
SMOKER
ROASTING PAN WITH RACK

Serves 4

1 To make the dry rub, place the sugar, dry mustard, pimentón, garlic powder, sea salt, ground cumin, ground peppercorns, black pepper, chili powder, and cayenne in a large metal bowl, put on a pair of rubber gloves, and toss everything well using your hands.

2 Place the ribs in a glass baking dish—a lasagna dish is perfect—and, using your hands, massage the rub into the meat on all sides. Don't hesitate to go overboard. Cover the dish with plastic wrap and refrigerate for 24 hours.

3 Remove the ribs from the refrigerator, loosen the plastic wrap, and let them come to room temperature. Meanwhile, soak 6 cups of good-quality hickory chips in water for at least an hour prior to starting the ribs.

4 If your smoker box is attached to your grill, turn it to medium and add about a cup of the soaked wood chips. Turn the left-most burner to medium and place the ribs on the grill grate over indirect heat. Close the grill lid and maintain the grill at a steady temperature of about 275°F–300°F for 1 hour.

5 After an hour, add another cup of the soaked wood chips to the smoker and continue to cook the ribs for another hour. If the wood chips seem to be burning too quickly, turn the temperature of the smoker down a bit. Continue to add chips for another 3 hours, turning the ribs after 1½ hours on the grill.

6 Preheat the oven to 350°F. Transfer the ribs to a platter and let them come to room temperature. Place a rack in a small metal roasting pan and fill the pan a quarter of the way with water. Place the ribs on the rack. Cover tightly with foil and place in the oven to steam for 30 minutes.

7 Remove the ribs from the oven and place them back on the grill over medium heat for another 30 minutes, turning them frequently. Serve warm, with bowls of your favorite sweet sauce on the side—and a lot of napkins.

VENISON MEATBALL SLIDERS

From Jon Bonnell, Bonnell's,
Fort Worth

This is an easy way to get everyone in your family to enjoy venison, especially for those who might be a little squeamish. These great little one-handed slider meatballs, which combine the slightly sweet, gamey meat with more familiar pork shoulder, are perfect for tailgates or around the campfire; the pork adds tenderness and a bit of luscious fat to the extremely lean venison. And with their rich sauce, the meatballs can also be served on spaghetti with some grated Parmesan. For quality venison, chef Jon Bonnell sources from the Hughes family at Broken Arrow Ranch based in the Texas Hill Country. Broken Arrow humanely harvests wild antelope and deer from more than one hundred Central and South Texas ranches spread out over a million combined acres. This is truly free-range meat, medication-and hormone-free and very low in fat.

Edible Tip

The meatballs can be pan-fried. Coat the bottom of a large, heavy skillet with vegetable oil and heat to medium-high. Once the oil is hot, fry the meatballs in batches until brown on all sides, 5–6 minutes.

1 LB VENISON MEAT, WITH FAT AND SILVERSKIN REMOVED, CUBED
½ LB PORK SHOULDER, CUBED
1 SHALLOT, MINCED
4 CLOVES GARLIC, MINCED
6 TBSP FRESHLY GRATED PARMESAN CHEESE
⅓ CUP PANKO BREADCRUMBS
1 TBSP CHOPPED FRESH PARSLEY
1 TBSP CHOPPED FRESH BASIL
½ TBSP CHOPPED FRESH OREGANO
1 TSP KOSHER SALT
½ TSP FRESHLY GROUND BLACK PEPPER
1½ TBSP DIJON MUSTARD

2 EGGS, BEATEN
VEGETABLE OIL FOR FRYING
MARINARA SAUCE (RECIPE ON PAGE 108), WARM
14 SLIDER BUNS OR SMALL ROLLS
GRATED MOZZARELLA CHEESE (OPTIONAL)

SPECIAL EQUIPMENT:
MEAT GRINDER (OR ASK YOUR LOCAL BUTCHER TO GRIND THE MEATS FOR YOU)

Makes about 10 sliders

1 Grind the pork and venison together through the smallest plate on your grinder and place the ground meat in a large bowl. Sprinkle in the shallot, garlic, Parmesan, breadcrumbs, herbs, salt, and pepper, and mix into the meat with your hands. Blend in the mustard and beaten eggs until everything is well mixed. Form into 2-ounce (golf-ball size) meatballs by rolling between your hands. If you have a kitchen scale, weighing each meatball is the most accurate way of making sure each one is the same size.

2 In a large Dutch oven, heat 2 inches of vegetable oil to 350°F over medium-high heat. Deep-fry the meatballs in batches for 1 minute. Place the cooked meatballs on a few layers of paper towels to absorb the excess oil.

3 Place the fried meatballs in the pot of marinara sauce and simmer for 15–20 minutes.

4 Serve the meatballs on slider buns or small rolls with an extra spoonful of sauce for each one and a sprinkling of mozzarella if you like.

MARINARA SAUCE

*From John Bonnell, Bonnell's,
Fort Worth*

Juicy tomatoes and fresh herbs are the pivotal ingredients for this classic Italian red sauce. It was the Spanish explorers of the mid-16th century who introduced the European palate to the tomato, a New World fruit first cultivated by the Aztecs. The word "marinara" is derived from the Italian word *marinaio,* or sailor. Some say this simple but flavorful sauce was devised by the wives of Neapolitan fishermen, who would make it quickly when their sea-faring husbands returned at the end of the day without a fresh catch. Marinara sauce is the building base for several more complex Italian red sauces, such as "puttanesca" and "arrabbiata." This version, created by chef Jon Bonnell for his Venison Meatball Sliders (page 107), can also be used in our Swiss Chard Lasagna (page 89) and the Cevola Family Eggplant Parmigiana (page 103).

3 TBSP OLIVE OIL
1 MEDIUM YELLOW ONION, CHOPPED
3 CLOVES GARLIC, MINCED
2 STALKS CELERY, CHOPPED
½ CUP DRY RED WINE
4 CUPS CANNED ITALIAN PLUM TOMATOES, CHOPPED, JUICES INCLUDED

2 TSP CHOPPED FRESH OREGANO
1 TSP CHOPPED FRESH BASIL
½ TSP CHOPPED FRESH THYME
1 TSP KOSHER SALT
PINCH OF FRESHLY GROUND BLACK PEPPER

Makes 4 cups

1 Heat the olive oil in a large saucepan over medium heat and sauté the onion, garlic, and celery until soft. Deglaze the pan with the wine and reduce the liquid until the pan is almost dry. Add the tomatoes and simmer for 8 minutes. Puree with an immersion blender until smooth or transfer to a regular blender and blend in batches. Stir in the herbs, salt, and pepper and simmer for another 3–5 minutes. Keep warm.

TEXAS CHILI CON CARNE

From Kelly Yandell,
TheMeaningofPie.com

Chili, the official dish of Texas, has evolved over hundreds of years. A small group of Canary Islanders settled in San Antonio in the early 1700s, bringing with them their spicy stews seasoned with cumin, garlic, and chiles. In the 1800s, their descendants, the Chili Queens, began serving their versions, each with its own secret ingredients, from open-air stalls at the *mercado* on San Antonio's Military Plaza. On cattle drives, chili was a standard dish for chuck wagon cooks, who planted herbs and peppers along the trail routes for future use. A Texas chili stand at the 1893 World's Fair in Chicago gave the rest of the states a taste, after which many varieties began to spring up around the country. Today most cooks use chili powder as a shortcut, but this recipe uses whole dried chiles, which can be found in many neighborhood grocery stores. Each brand of chili powder contains a different mix of chiles and seasonings. By using dried whole peppers, you can determine which chile nuances suit your tastes and eventually devise your own blend.

Edible Tip

- If you are unable to monitor the chili closely, this recipe can be cooked on a slow braise in the oven. Preheat the oven to 225°F and cook for 2 hours before adding the masa paste. After adding the masa, return the chili to the oven for another 30 minutes.

3 ANCHO CHILES

3 DRIED DE ARBOL CHILES

1 DRIED JAPONÉS CHILES

3 JALAPEÑOS, STEMS AND SEEDS REMOVED (WEAR RUBBER GLOVES)

2 HEAPING TSP GROUND CUMIN

4 CLOVES GARLIC, PEELED

1 (28 OZ) CAN WHOLE TOMATOES, WITH JUICE

1 ONION, QUARTERED

1 TSP DRIED OREGANO, PREFERABLY MEXICAN

2 TSP SALT

3–3½ LB SIRLOIN TIPS, COARSELY GROUND FOR CHILI

¼ CUP CORN MASA FLOUR

SHREDDED CHEDDAR CHEESE AND CHOPPED ONIONS FOR GARNISH (OPTIONAL)

Serves 4–5

1 To prepare the dried chiles wearing rubber gloves, cut each of them open and discard the seeds and any membranes that are easily removed. Place the chiles in a small pan with just enough water to cover them. Over medium heat, simmer the chiles and water for 15 minutes. Remove the chiles from the water, reserving the water, and transfer to a food processor.

2 Add the jalapeños, cumin, garlic, tomatoes (with their juice), onion, oregano, and salt to the food processor. Process until smooth.

3 In a large stockpot, combine the meat and the tomato-chile puree. Add just enough water (not the reserved chile water) to cover the meat, and bring to a simmer over medium heat. Cover the pot and cook for 1½ hours. If necessary, add more water, just enough to keep the meat covered.

4 After 1½ hours, mix the masa flour with enough water to make a smooth paste. Slowly add the mixture to the chili while stirring. Simmer the chili over very low heat for another 30 minutes, stirring occasionally.

5 Taste the chili and season as necessary with salt and the reserved chile water. Serve with shredded cheddar cheese and onions if you like.

JON AND WENDY TAGGART

Burgundy Pasture Beef, Grandview

At the point of the herd, a white and brown dappled longhorn named Lightning trots across the open pasture toward a holding pen. Trailing closely behind the majestic lead steer is an orderly procession of Black Angus heifers. Jon Taggart, riding in his Kubota RTV, rounds up the stragglers from the back and sides. The scene is calm, and Lightning and Taggart make a striking pair working in tandem, as they've done for ten years.

Even without his horse, fifty-four-year-old Taggart is every bit the traditional cowboy: a long, lanky frame (six-foot-five minus hat), a silver mustache, an unmistakable Texas drawl, and a wit to match. "My father didn't know the eating end of a cow from the pooping end," he says, looking out across the fourteen-hundred-acre spread that is home to Burgundy Pasture Beef.

Ranching may not have been in his blood, but Taggart, a Fort Worth native, graduated in 1979 from Texas A&M, a university revered for its school of agriculture. Coming full circle, he recently returned to his alma mater to speak at a seminar devoted to grass-fed beef. Texas is the cradle of the cattle country, but the state is still in

its infancy when it comes to embracing sustainable practices again. When he switched to grass-fed methods twelve years ago, other ranchers, many of them ex-classmates, were skeptical. "If they didn't say I was crazy, you could damn sure tell by the look in their eyes and the tone of their voice," says Taggart.

His grazing pastures are now filled with scores of native grasses that mature and rotate naturally with the seasons. "Some have roots twenty feet deep," he explains, then reels off their names and attributes like familiar friends—little bluestem, big bluestem, Indian grass, kleingrass, clover, and side oats grama. Grama is the state grass of Texas. Switchgrass, he says, is like ice cream to cows. "See over there," he says, pointing across the fence line. "My neighbor's field is a monoculture. They make hay. The other day, his ground temperature was 110 degrees. Mine was 80 degrees. The grasses in my pastures survive tough conditions and require no farming. Economically, that makes great sense."

"Jon's a free thinker," says his wife, Wendy, during lunch at Burgundy Beef's storefront and grill in Grandview about fifteen minutes down

the road. "Often, agriculture is based on doing what your daddy did. Jon didn't have to worry about family traditions." Wendy, a petite woman with a pretty face and cropped, sun-streaked hair, manages the butchering and marketing end of their operation. In college, she was granted a full scholarship to study agriculture but ultimately majored in business. "Jon takes care of the cattle while they're alive," she says with a grin. "And I take care of them when they're not."

They raise Black Angus, an Old World breed with a moderate frame and genetics that make for nicely marbled beef. The Taggarts have built an on-site USDA-approved butchering facility, where a staff of six provides quality cutting and packaging for Burgundy Pasture Beef as well as a growing number of other producers.

The Taggarts make weekly deliveries to an impressive list of restaurants and private homes around the Dallas–Fort Worth metroplex. "We're helping to create change," says Wendy. "There are mornings when you're so tired, and then a customer calls to tell you how much they loved your meat. That's when you know it's all worth it."

SLOW-BRAISED CHUCK ROAST

From Jon and Wendy Taggart,
Burgundy Pasture Beef, Grandview

Chuck roast is a classic braising cut, with lots of flavor and nutrition. Braising means long, slow cooking. Wendy and Jon Taggart of Burgundy Pasture Beef suggest two rules that will always yield good results: don't cook at a high temperature (stay below 300°F) and make sure the meat has ample protection to hold in moisture while braising. Whether you're cooking on a stove top, in an oven, in a slow cooker, or on a smoker, these rules hold.

Edible Tip

To make the bouquet garni, place 1 bay leaf, 1 sprig fresh rosemary, 3 sprigs fresh oregano, and 5 sprigs fresh thyme in a piece of cheesecloth, and tie it closed with kitchen twine.

3 LB CHUCK ROAST (BONE IN OR OUT)
2 TSP KOSHER SALT OR SEA SALT
1 TSP COARSELY GROUND BLACK PEPPER
2 TSP FINELY CHOPPED GARLIC
1 TBSP OLIVE OIL
1 CUP CHOPPED ONION
¾ CUP CHOPPED CELERY
½ CUP RED WINE
½ CUP BEEF STOCK
1 BOUQUET GARNI
1 TBSP UNSALTED BUTTER (OPTIONAL)

Serves 6

1 Rub the roast with the salt, pepper, and garlic. Cover and let stand at room temperature 1–2 hours.

2 Preheat the oven to 225°F. Set a large, preferably cast-iron Dutch oven over medium-high heat. When it begins to smoke, carefully drizzle in the olive oil. Brown the roast on all sides, about 7–9 minutes per side, until it has a rich brown crust all over. Transfer the roast to a platter.

3 Add the onion and celery to the pot and stir well, cooking until the onion is translucent. Add the wine and stock, bring to a boil, and reduce the liquid by about a quarter. Reduce the heat to a low simmer and add the roast back to the pan.

4 Place a piece of aluminum foil over the top of the pot. (This will create a tighter seal, holding the moisture in.) Cover the foil with the pot lid. Place the roast in the oven and cook until fork-tender, about 4 hours.

5 The slowly braised roast produces wonderful meat juices. After removing the roast from the pan, these can be further reduced for a jus to be poured back over the roast. If desired after reducing, add the butter, and stir until melted.

MARY'S SAUCY SKILLET STEAK

*From Robert Hutchins,
Rehoboth Ranch, Greenville*

Because grass-fed beef is leaner than corn-fed meat, be careful not to overcook it. The Hutchins family loves the way eldest daughter, Mary, simmers the meat in its own juices. A top hand in the kitchen since she was twelve, Mary prepared meals for the family of fourteen until she married and started her own family. Rarely one to use a recipe, Mary was persuaded to write down her Saucy Skillet Steak so the family could share it with customers.

¼ CUP KETCHUP
1 TBSP WORCESTERSHIRE SAUCE
¼ TSP SALT
½ TSP DRIED MARJORAM
½ TSP RED PEPPER FLAKES
¼ TSP FRESHLY GROUND BLACK PEPPER
1 LB 1½-INCH-THICK STEAK (TOP ROUND OR SIRLOIN)
¼ CUP UNBLEACHED ALL-PURPOSE FLOUR

1 TBSP OLIVE OIL
1 LARGE ONION, CHOPPED
¼ CUP CHOPPED RED BELL PEPPER
1 (10 OZ) PACKAGE FROZEN ITALIAN GREEN BEANS
1 (2 OZ) JAR SLICED PIMIENTO, DRAINED
RICE, MASHED POTATOES, OR COUSCOUS FOR SERVING

Serves 4

1 In a small bowl, mix together the ketchup, Worcestershire, salt, marjoram, red pepper flakes, and black pepper; set aside.

2 Coat the steak with the flour. Using a meat tenderizer mallet, pound the flour into the steak.

3 Place a heavy skillet large enough to hold the steak over medium-high heat and heat the olive oil until it begins to shimmer but not smoke. Brown the steak in the hot oil for 3–4 minutes per side, searing it to form a crust before turning it over. Use tongs to transfer the seared beef onto a plate.

4 Add the onion and bell pepper to the pan and cook and stir until the onion is translucent and the pepper is tender, about 5 minutes. Add 1 cup water and stir in the ketchup mixture. Bring to a boil, and then reduce the heat to low. Return the steak to the skillet. Cover and simmer until the steak is tender, 70–90 minutes.

5 Rinse the frozen green beans under running cold water to separate. Add the beans and drained pimientos to the skillet. Let simmer until the green beans are heated through, about 10 minutes. Serve over rice, mashed potatoes, or couscous.

MEAT AND BAMIA STEW

*From Mary Karish, Garden Chair,
Coppell Community Garden*

Mary Karish is a master gardener and citrus specialist who is part of the volunteer force that oversees the Coppell Community Garden. She also gives presentations to gardeners on how to grow fruits and vegetables organically. It may be surprising to learn that the Lebanese were among the many immigrant groups that came to Texas in the early twentieth century. This dish from Karish's homeland takes advantage of two of Texas's favorite homegrown vegetables, tomatoes and okra. "Lamb was always used in the past," Karish says, "but today, many families prefer to make it with beef." That's an easy order for North Texas's growing community of grass-fed beef growers.

Edible Tip

Pomegranate concentrate can be found in the ethnic section of most supermarkets or in Middle Eastern stores. Coconut oil can be found in any good Asian or Indian supermarket.

2 LB FRESH OKRA (BAMIA)
6 TBSP COLD-PRESSED COCONUT OIL
2 LB GRASS-FED STEWING BEEF OR LAMB, CUT INTO 2-INCH CHUNKS
2 LB RIPE TOMATOES, JUICED (ABOUT 2 CUPS PULPY LIQUID)
⅓ TSP FRESHLY GROUND BLACK PEPPER
½ TSP GROUND CINNAMON
¼ TSP CAYENNE (OPTIONAL)
1–2 TBSP TOMATO PASTE

1 LARGE HEAD GARLIC, CLOVES PEELED AND FINELY MINCED
LEAVES FROM 1 BUNCH FRESH CILANTRO, CHOPPED (¾–1 CUP)
SALT
JUICE OF 1 LEMON
3 TBSP UNSWEETENED POMEGRANATE CONCENTRATE
HOT COOKED RICE FOR SERVING

Serves 4–6

1 Wash and dry the okra and trim off the stems.

2 Heat 2 tablespoons of the coconut oil in a large skillet over medium-low heat. Sauté the okra until it begins to caramelize and turn golden brown. Set aside.

3 Heat 2 tablespoons of the coconut oil in a 5-quart cast-iron Dutch oven over medium-high heat. When it shimmers and is hot, brown the meat chunks on all sides. Reduce the heat to low, add the tomato liquid, cover the pot, and simmer until the meat is almost tender but still a little chewy, 1–1½ hours.

4 Add the okra, pepper, cinnamon, cayenne, and tomato paste to the meat, stirring well to combine. Heat the remaining 2 tablespoons coconut oil in a skillet over medium-low heat and sauté the garlic until it's translucent gold, about 5 minutes. Fold in the cilantro, then stir mixture into the stew and simmer another 30 minutes, until the meat is completely tender.

5 Season to taste with salt and add the lemon juice and pomegranate concentrate. Stir slowly to mix without breaking the okra until the flavors are blended, about 5 minutes. Serve over the cooked rice.

GRILLED NEW YORK STRIP

From John Stout, Celebration Restaurant, Dallas

For restaurant-quality grilled steak, all you need is little salt, pepper, and garlic powder and a great piece of meat, according to chef John Stout at Celebration Restaurant. Stout buys 100 percent grass-fed steaks from Burgundy Pasture Beef in Grandview, where Jon and Wendy Taggart raise their Angus cattle on a diet of lush native grasses. The Taggarts even have their own *boucherie*, or butcher's market, adding another element of freshness and quality to the cuts they're bringing to the market. Here, Stout shares the incredibly simple method he uses to enhance the meat's inherent flavors. The spices can be adjusted to individual taste. The very first goal of grilling a steak is a good sear on the meat, so get your backyard grill hot and ready to go.

Edible Tips

• Make sure you allow the steaks adequate resting time after removing them from the grill. This time is critical to let the meat redistribute and reabsorb moisture that is pushed toward the center of the meat during cooking. If you cut the steak too soon, all of the delicious juices run out onto the plate.

• If you cook steak often, prepare a large batch of the seasoning salt and keep it in a shaker jar so you are ready to go at any time.

1 TSP KOSHER SALT
½ TSP FINELY GROUND BLACK PEPPER
¼ TSP GRANULATED GARLIC

2 (10 OZ) NEW YORK STRIP STEAKS, 1¼ INCHES THICK, AT ROOM TEMPERATURE

Serves 2

1 Preheat the grill to high, 450°F on a gas grill.

2 In a small bowl, combine the salt, pepper, and granulated garlic. Set aside.

3 Place the steaks on the hottest part of the grill and let cook without moving for 2 minutes. Without flipping the steaks, turn them 45 degrees, so that you can achieve nice crosshatch sear marks. Allow the steaks to cook an additional 30 seconds on that side without moving.

4 Flip the steaks over and sprinkle them with the seasoned salt. Allow them to cook for another 2½ minutes.

5 Remove the steaks to a plate and tent loosely with aluminum foil. Allow the steaks to rest for a minimum of 6 minutes before serving.

MAINS

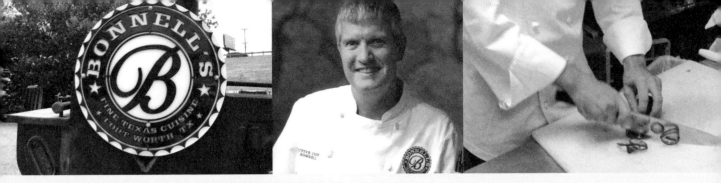

JON BONNELL,

Bonnell's Fine Texas Cuisine, Fort Worth

To some folks, it might seem odd to read the terms *fine dining* and *Texas* in the same sentence. And *cuisine*, well, that word might be a little fancy for some Fort Worth old-timers. But for Jon Bonnell, a fourth-generation Texan, the juxtaposition is exactly the concept he intended for his namesake restaurant.

Why not serve juicy ribs and sopping sauce over linen tablecloths or venison sliders by candlelight? And why not gussy up traditional Mexican favorites like fire-roasted chiles rellenos with a stuffing of local chèvre (translation: goat cheese) and cilantro pesto?

Though Bonnell's tasty food is indeed "Fine Texas Cuisine," the restaurant would be packed regardless of what it served, because Jon Bonnell is one of the best-liked chefs in the entire state. While sipping my Dublin (Texas) Dr Pepper float at the bar, I quiz a few regulars on a busy weekday night about Bonnell's the restaurant, Jon the man, and the differences between dining in Dallas and dining in Fort Worth.

"Come here often?" I ask one of my bar mates. "Yep, been here hundreds of times," he answers, offering me one of his Oysters Texasfeller. He tells me how much he admires Jon, and clearly, he loves the food. Overhearing our conversation, several others chime in. "Great chefs succeed in Fort Worth if they're friendly and humble," they tell me. "Jon is all that and more. In Dallas, restaurants are trendier. Our restaurants serve comfort foods, foods that are more traditional."

As I sit with Jon in the foyer the next day, we laugh about the rivalry between our two North Texas cities.

Like Australians and New Zealanders, Norwegians and Swedes, Fort Worthians and Dallasites are generically Texans to the outside world, but we do have our differences as well as similarities, like the pride we share in our heritage. Using local farmers and ranchers for regional Texas cuisine is a no-brainer for Jon Bonnell.

He's just purchased a box of Eight-Ball squash at Cowtown Farmers Market and, on the fly, he's stuffing them with Texas venison, orzo rice, pine nuts, and herbs for one of tonight's specials. He shows me photos on his iPhone of the new farmers he's just met. He wants to remember the faces with the names.

"Look at this," he says, showing me his contact list. Under cheeses, he has ten local purveyors. "We're using six right now, but as the menu changes, we'll rotate."

As we discuss the wonderful local cheddars of the Veldhuizen family, an older gentleman walks by, as if on cue, wearing a T-shirt emblazoned with the words *Veldhuizen Cheese*. Jon jumps up and engages him in conversation. The man recently visited the dairy farm and liked their cheeses. Today is his first visit to Bonnell's.

"I'm a longtime vegetarian," he says, "but as I've gotten older, I've lost muscle mass. I heard that Bonnell's grass-fed beef and buffalo were the best in town. Thought I'd give it a try."

Jon introduces himself as the Bonnell in Bonnell's, and the man is impressed. "I'm honored. I'll be back for more protein next week," he says. Jon grins and shakes his hand. "I'll look forward to it." And he really means it.

RED CHILE BRAISED SHORT RIBS

From Jon Bonnell,
Bonnell's, Fort Worth

Short ribs are one of the most flavorful cuts in the entire butcher case, according to chef Jon Bonnell, the Cowtown expert on cooking pasture-raised Texas beef. But short ribs also require slow-cooking techniques to make them tender. "This is one of those dishes that takes a little work at first," says Bonnell, "but after that, it goes into the oven for five hours and comes out perfect every time." A complex sauce forms when the natural juices of the short ribs combine with the earthy chiles. It's a hearty gravy that begs for a thick slice of bread or a dinner roll for sopping.

1 TBSP UNSALTED BUTTER
1 YELLOW ONION, DICED
2 STALKS CELERY, DICED
5 CLOVES GARLIC, CHOPPED
3 DRIED CASCABEL CHILES
3 DRIED GUAJILLO CHILES
3 DRIED PASILLA CHILES
1 DRIED ANCHO CHILE
2 TBSP TOMATO PASTE
3½ CUPS CHICKEN STOCK
2½ TSP KOSHER SALT

½ TSP CRACKED BLACK
    PEPPERCORNS
¼ TSP GROUND CORIANDER
½ TSP SMOKED PAPRIKA
1 (4-INCH) CINNAMON STICK
PINCH OF GROUND CUMIN
8 THICK-CUT LARGE BEEF SHORT RIBS
1 TBSP VEGETABLE OIL
½ CUP DRY RED WINE

Serves 8

1 Preheat the oven to 250°F.

2 In a heavy soup pot over medium heat, melt the butter and sauté the onion, celery, and garlic until the onion softens.

3 Remove and discard the stems and seeds from the dried chiles, and add them to the pot. Stir in the tomato paste and pour in the stock, and then add 1½ teaspoons of the salt and the pepper, coriander, paprika, cinnamon stick, and cumin. Reduce the heat to low and simmer, covered, for 1 hour.

4 Remove the cinnamon stick. Using an immersion blender, carefully puree the entire mixture until smooth. Strain the sauce through a fine-mesh strainer.

5 Sprinkle the short ribs generously with the remaining 1 teaspoon salt. In a Dutch oven over high heat, heat the oil until it just begins to smoke, and then carefully brown the short ribs on all sides. Once the ribs are brown and caramelized, deglaze the pot with the wine, scraping all the browned bits from the bottom of the pot. Then pour in the chile sauce and cover with a tight-fitting lid.

6 Place the pot in the oven and cook until the meat falls off the bones, about 5 hours. Serve the ribs one to a person, with a generous portion of sauce.

GRILLED GULF SHRIMP AND VEGETABLE SALAD

From Kent Rathbun, Rathbun's Blue Plate Kitchen, Dallas

Texans love to barbecue, but don't think beef is the only thing on the grill. This colorful mix of grilled vegetables and fresh Gulf shrimp tossed in a garlicky Champagne vinaigrette makes a light, healthy main course. The stars in chef Kent Rathbun's galaxy of restaurant successes include Jasper's, Abacus, and Rathbun's Blue Plate Kitchen, the latter of which draws its inspiration from family recipes and regional purveyors. The atmosphere is casual and the menu is homespun, but there's still that touch of Rathbun elegance.

FOR THE DRESSING:

¼ CUP OLIVE OIL

4 CLOVES GARLIC, CHOPPED

2 SHALLOTS, MINCED

¼ CUP CHAMPAGNE VINEGAR

1 TSP CRACKED BLACK PEPPERCORNS

2 TBSP CHOPPED FRESH BASIL

1 TBSP CHOPPED FRESH OREGANO

JUICE OF 2 LEMONS

1 TSP KOSHER SALT

FOR THE SALAD:

1 LARGE CARROT, PEELED, SLICED INTO ROUNDS ⅛ INCH THICK, BLANCHED, AND CHILLED

2 LARGE PORTOBELLO MUSHROOMS, QUARTERED

1 LARGE RED BELL PEPPER, SEEDED AND QUARTERED

1 LARGE YELLOW BELL PEPPER, SEEDED QUARTERED

1 LARGE GREEN BELL PEPPER, SEEDED AND QUARTERED

1 LARGE YELLOW SQUASH, SLICED INTO ROUNDS ¼ INCH THICK

1 LARGE ZUCCHINI, SLICED INTO ROUNDS ¼ INCH THICK

8 GREEN ONIONS

1 LARGE RED ONION, SLICED INTO ROUNDS ¼ INCH THICK

2 HEADS RADICCHIO, QUARTERED

½ CUP EXTRA-VIRGIN OLIVE OIL

1 TBSP CRACKED BLACK PEPPERCORNS

1 TBSP KOSHER SALT

1 LB (16–20 COUNT) EXTRA-LARGE SHRIMP, PEELED AND DEVEINED

¼ CUP CANOLA OIL

SPRIGS FRESH BASIL FOR THE GARNISH

SPECIAL EQUIPMENT:

A 10– BY 12–INCH GRILL BASKET

Serves 4

MAKE THE DRESSING:

1 In a small bowl, whisk together the olive oil, garlic, shallots, and vinegar. Add the pepper, basil, oregano, lemon juice, and salt, and whisk again to combine and emulsify. Cover and set aside at room temperature while you prepare the vegetables and shrimp.

MAKE THE SALAD:

2 Before starting the grill fire, clean the grates very well and brush with a very small amount of vegetable oil. Start the fire about 1 hour before you plan to cook. Use good-quality charcoal with hickory or mesquite chips. Allow the coals to get completely white before starting to grill.

3 While waiting for the grill to heat, combine the carrot, mushrooms, bell peppers, squash, green onions, red onion, and radicchio in a large bowl. Pour the olive oil over the vegetables and season with the cracked pepper and 1½ teaspoons of the salt. Use tongs to completely coat all the vegetables with the oil and seasonings. Cover and set aside at room temperature.

4 In a large bowl, toss the shrimp in the canola oil and the remaining 1½ teaspoons salt, cover, and place in the refrigerator.

5 Put marinated vegetables in a grill basket and place on the grill. Grill 4 to 5 minutes on one side, flip basket over, and grill for another 4 or 5 minutes, until vegetables soften and grill marks are apparent on both sides. When complete, remove the basket and set aside. Next, place the shrimp on the grill and cook for 2 minutes, flip, and grill another 2–3 minutes.

6 Remove shrimp and arrange with the vegetables on a large platter. Dress with vinaigrette, garnish with basil sprigs, and serve.

GULF REDFISH WITH ARTICHOKE BARIGOULE AND TUSCAN SALSA VERDE

*From Graham Dodds, Hotel Palomar,
formerly with Bolsa, Dallas*

Many thought of redfish as "trash fish," until chef Paul Prudhomme introduced blackened redfish to the culinary mainstream in the 1980s. Now it is one of the Gulf's most popular catches for sport fishermen. Also known as red drum and identified by a distinctive black dot on its tail, redfish is a medium-textured whitefish with a firm flake. In this recipe, chef Graham Dodds coats the fillets with an herbal rub and then quickly pan sears them before baking. They are topped with a Mediterranean salsa verde made of herbs, capers, and olive oil and presented over an artichoke barigoule, a Provençal dish of artichokes stewed in white wine.

FOR THE BARIGOULE:
¼ CUP OLIVE OIL
1 MEDIUM YELLOW ONION, DICED
1 FENNEL BULB, DICED
½ CUP CHICKEN STOCK
2 CUPS SAUVIGNON BLANC
¼ CUP FRESH LEMON JUICE
1 CUP BLANCHED AND QUARTERED
  FRESH ARTICHOKE HEARTS
  OR 2 (6 OZ) JARS QUARTERED
  ARTICHOKE HEARTS PACKED
  IN WATER, WELL DRAINED AND
  RINSED
2 TBSP SALTED BUTTER
1 TBSP FINELY CHOPPED FRESH
  BASIL
1 TBSP FINELY CHOPPED FRESH
  CHIVES
1 TBSP FINELY CHOPPED FRESH
  FLAT-LEAF PARSLEY
KOSHER SALT
WHITE PEPPER

FOR THE SALSA VERDE:
2 CUPS FINELY CHOPPED FRESH
  FLAT-LEAF PARSLEY
1 CUP FINELY CHOPPED FRESH
  CILANTRO

½ CUP FINELY CHOPPED FRESH
  BASIL
2 TBSP CAPERS, RINSED AND DRIED
1 TBSP DIJON MUSTARD
RED PEPPER FLAKES
SALT
PINCH OF SUGAR
¾ CUP EXTRA-VIRGIN OLIVE OIL
  (USE LESS AT FIRST AND ADD
  MORE IF NEEDED)

FOR THE FISH:
½ CUP FINELY CHOPPED FRESH
  FLAT-LEAF PARSLEY
⅓ CUP FINELY CHOPPED FRESH
  CHIVES
⅓ CUP FINELY CHOPPED FRESH
  BASIL
4 REDFISH FILLETS (6–7 OZ EACH),
  SKIN REMOVED
¼ CUP OLIVE OIL
KOSHER SALT
FRESHLY GROUND BLACK PEPPER

Serves 4

START THE BARIGOULE:
1 In a large stainless steel saucepan, heat the olive oil over medium-high heat. Add the onion and fennel and stir constantly until soft but not brown, about 5 minutes. Add the stock, wine, and lemon juice and cook over medium heat until the liquid is reduced by half. Stir in the artichokes, cover, and set aside at room temperature.

MAKE THE SALSA VERDE:
2 Combine the herbs, capers, mustard, red pepper flakes, salt to taste, sugar, and olive oil in a blender (not a food processor, which will shred the herbs). Slowly pulse and then blend until smooth. (Don't run the blender too long or it will heat up the sauce and turn it brown.) Set aside.

EDIBLE DALLAS & FORT WORTH: THE COOKBOOK

120

PREPARE AND COOK THE FISH:

3 Preheat the oven to 400°F. In a medium bowl, combine the herbs. Rub the herb mixture into both sides of the fish fillets.

4 Coat the bottom of a large ovenproof skillet with the olive oil and heat over medium-high heat until it begins to shimmer. Add the fish and brown 1 minute on each side. Put the skillet in the oven until the fish is cooked through (about 8 minutes). Season to taste with salt and black pepper.

FINISH THE BARIGOULE:

5 Once the fish goes into the oven, uncover the artichokes, bring to a boil over medium-high heat, and stir in the butter and herbs. Reduce the heat to low and cook until the butter is melted. Season to taste with salt and white pepper.

ASSEMBLE THE DISH:

6 On each plate, spoon one-quarter of the barigoule. Place a redfish fillet on top of the barigoule and spoon the salsa verde over the fish. Serve immediately.

GRAHAM DODDS

Hotel Palomar, formerly with Bolsa, Dallas

Seasonal and local is more than a marketing mantra for Chef Graham Dodds, recognized by the *Dallas Morning News* as one of Dallas–Fort Worth's top new chefs in 2008. Dodds traces his reverence for the earth and its creatures to the childhood summers he spent with his grandparents in the north of England.

"My parents sent me there for speech therapy," he laughs. "They thought they could prevent a Texas accent. My grandfather was a proud Scotsman and a hobby beekeeper. My grandmother had a kitchen garden with fruit trees, berries, and a field of flowers."

His parents met at the University of St. Andrews and came to the States for his father's job with Bell Helicopter. "They wanted to get away from the rain, so they moved to California but eventually ended up in Texas," says Dodds.

The taste of the raw honey from his grandfather's hives stayed with him, and Dodds eventually began maintaining his own hives in Texas. "Texas can be a harsh landscape during the heat of the summer for both bees and farmers," he says, chopping a line of baby carrots from Eden Creek Farm, where several of his hives are located.

Farm owners Steve and Kristine Orth are longtime friends, and they provide Dodds with lots of fresh produce for his creations. Dodds knows of their farm's struggles and triumphs. A tornado damaged several of their structures in April, and now there are triple-digit temperatures and no rain.

"Steve and Kristine also raise heritage-breed Red Wattle hogs," says Dodds. "The hogs roam free, eating

wild plums, persimmons, and dewberries around the farm. I've never had bacon so good in my life. It's the most amazing pork."

Dodds studied art in college but cooked to supplement his income. "I suppose what I'm doing now is a form of art," he says. "Temporary, edible

art . . . but still art." His early culinary experiences were spent in some of Dallas's most innovative kitchens, like Stephan Pyles's Star Canyon. He moved to Portland to attend the Western Culinary Institute and found work with Greg Higgins at his newly opened downtown restaurant. It was here Dodds got one of his most memorable lessons on what it means to be seasonal.

"It was 1994 and Higgins had Portland's best burger with one hundred percent local ingredients. When it was winter, he refused to put a tomato on it, no matter how loudly customers complained. He'd just shake his head and say, 'Tomatoes don't grow in Portland this time of year.'"

Dodds furthered his education in sustainability during the three years he spent at the Inn at Shelburne Farms in Vermont, a historic fourteen-hundred-acre working farm on the shores of Lake Champlain. "We made our own cheddar and collected maple syrup, had a two-acre market garden, and raised our own lamb, beef, and pork. I did the butchering. You gain a real respect for animals when your meat doesn't come out of a shrink-wrapped bag. To overcook something meant wasting an animal's life. My time in Vermont made me mindful of that."

SHRIMP IN WHITE WINE
SAUCE OVER PASTA

From Trellise Brennan, Brennan Vineyards, Comanche

Pat and Trellise Brennan, owners of Brennan Vineyards in Comanche, suggest you pair this buttery shrimp and pasta dish with their 2010 Viognier. In 2009, they poured their Viognier and Cabernet at the prestigious James Beard House in New York. "Tom and Lisa Perini (of Perini Ranch Steakhouse in Buffalo Gap) wanted Texas wines to pair with their cowboy cuisine, so they invited us," says Trellise. "The James Beard House is a New York brownstone with no elevators, which makes it interesting for the waitstaff because there are dining rooms on three floors." Brennan Vineyards is located near the geographic center of Texas at the junction of the state's most acclaimed wine grape regions, the Hill Country and the Texas High Plains. Dinners are held at the vineyard on the second Friday of each month except August, featuring chefs Steve Harris and Steven Puckett.

1 TSP KOSHER SALT
1 LB SPAGHETTI (PLAIN OR WHOLE WHEAT)
½ STICK (4 TBSP) UNSALTED BUTTER
6 TBSP OLIVE OIL
2 LB (26–30 COUNT) SHRIMP, PEELED AND DEVEINED
4 CLOVES GARLIC, CHOPPED
1 CUP BRENNAN VINEYARDS BUFFALO RHÔME BLANC OR A SAUVIGNON BLANC
⅓ CUP FRESH LEMON JUICE
½ TSP RED PEPPER FLAKES
½ TSP FRESHLY GROUND BLACK PEPPER
½ CUP CHOPPED FRESH PARSLEY
FRESHLY GRATED PARMESAN CHEESE FOR GARNISH

Serves 4

1 Fill a large stockpot with water and add the salt. Bring the water to a boil over high heat, drop in the pasta, and cook until al dente according to the package instructions. Drain and keep warm while you cook the shrimp.

2 In a 12- to 14-inch skillet over medium-high heat, heat 2 tablespoons of the butter with the olive oil until the butter melts. Add the shrimp, cook 1 minute on each side, and then add the garlic, wine, lemon juice, and red pepper and cook for 2 more minutes.

3 Add the cooked pasta to the skillet and toss gently with tongs. Stir in the black pepper, parsley, and remaining 2 tablespoons butter. Divide among 4 pasta bowls and serve with fresh-grated Parmesan if desired.

BLACK BEER–BOILED SPICED GULF SHRIMP

From Elissa Altman, Edible Communities, Inc.

Exactly what it claims to be, this simple, one-pot dish requires the following: a pound of unpeeled sweet Gulf shrimp, Old Bay seasoning, a few bottles of the best dark beer you can find, a porch, a summer afternoon, and a ton of napkins. For those of you who get a little wonky about having to mess with shrimp shells or veins, go ahead and clean them; if the shrimp are particularly small and it doesn't matter to you (it doesn't matter to us), you'll be rewarded for your bravery with the most tender and delectable spiced shrimp boil you've ever had.

2 (12 OZ) BOTTLES DARK BEER (STOUT OR PORTER, PREFERABLY A LOCAL TEXAS BEER)
2 TBSP OLD BAY SEASONING
¼ TSP CAYENNE

1 LB (26-30 COUNT) MEDIUM GULF SHRIMP, UNPEELED
1 LEMON, CUT INTO WEDGES

Serves 3–4

1 Bring the beer to a rolling simmer in a large saucepan over medium-high heat. Add the Old Bay seasoning and cayenne and continue to simmer for another 5 minutes. Add the shrimp and cook until pink, 3–5 minutes.

2 Remove the shrimp with a slotted spoon and serve with a squirt of lemon and a stack of napkins.

STUFFED ARTICHOKES

From Marie Tedei, Eden's Garden CSA Farm, Balch Springs

Artichokes, like asparagus, are a perennial: plant them once and enjoy them year after year. Most of those in the grocery's produce section come from California, but agricultural researchers with Texas A&M believe that the vegetable has commercial potential in certain parts of Texas where the mild winters and terrain are comparable to those in the Mediterranean region, where the artichoke originates. This recipe from Marie Tedei at Eden's Garden CSA Farm in Balch Springs was passed down from her Sicilian grandmother. "When cooking, my grandmother used the palms of her hands to measure ingredients," says Tedei. "I had to follow her around with a set of measuring spoons to learn how to prepare our family favorites." Serve this dish with a side of pasta and homemade red sauce. Eden's Garden CSA Farm is a fourteen-acre urban farm just twenty minutes from downtown Dallas. The farm produces organic produce for CSA members and also serves as a community teaching facility for visitors of all ages.

Edible Tip

• This is a finger food. The "meat" on the leaves should be tender enough to scrape off with your teeth. Serve in a bowl with a side plate for discarded outer leaves.

1 LB GRASS-FED GROUND BEEF
1 TSP MINCED YELLOW ONION
1 CLOVE GARLIC, CRUSHED
1 TSP DRIED OREGANO
2 TSP CHOPPED FRESH PARSLEY
½ CUP DRIED BREADCRUMBS
½ CUP GRATED ROMANO CHEESE
1 EGG
2 TBSP MILK
4 FRESH MEDIUM ARTICHOKES, RINSED AND DRAINED
1 LEMON WEDGE FOR RUBBING
1–2 TBSP OLIVE OIL, TEXAS OLIVE RANCH PREFERRED
2 TSP SALT OR TO TASTE

Serves 4

1 In a bowl, combine the ground beef, onion, garlic, oregano, 1 teaspoon of the parsley, the breadcrumbs, and the cheese. Mix the egg and milk in with your hands until the mixture is well blended. Cover the bowl and chill in the refrigerator for 1 hour.

2 With a serrated knife, cut off the stems and top quarter of each artichoke and discard. Trim the tips of the artichoke leaves and rub the lemon wedge over the cut surfaces (this will preserve color during cooking). Spread and loosen the leaves of the artichokes, making spaces between leaves with your fingers. Divide the meat mixture into 4 equal portions. Tuck one portion into the opened leaves of each artichoke.

3 Place the stuffed artichokes upright in a small Dutch oven, or similar covered pan just large enough so the artichokes can sit snugly upright. Drizzle olive oil over tops of the stuffed artichokes and slowly add water until the level reaches halfway up the sides of the artichokes. Cover the pot and bring the water to a boil over high heat. Immediately reduce the heat and simmer for about 1 hour, adding water as needed to keep the water level constant. The artichokes are done when the outer leaves pull off easily and the meat filling is cooked. Remove the artichokes from the water with a spatula and tongs to keep the leaves intact and place on a parchment paper-lined baking sheet.

4 Preheat the broiler and broil the artichokes until the meat crisps and browns a bit. Sprinkle with salt to taste and garnish with the remaining 1 teaspoon parsley before serving.

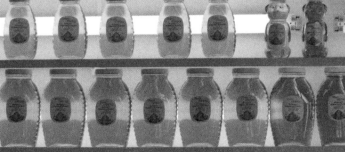

CHAPTER 5

DESSERTS AND DRINKS

Inspired by porch swings and family gardens, by the fragrant wafts from a grandmother's kitchen, and the memory of honey from a grandfather's beehive, these desserts and drinks are recipes with a history. North Texas berries, peaches, figs, and persimmons have staggered ripening dates from the spring into the fall. Pecans are also gathered in the fall. The midwinter days are brightened with the arrival of red grapefruit and sweet oranges from South Texas. There are recipes here for each season, like winter's warm apple-grapefruit cider and bourbon-soaked bread pudding or summer's black and blue lemonade and strawberries Romanoff. There's an old-fashioned chocolate cream pie and new-fashioned Turkish coffee truffles. Like a kid in a candy store, you'll be eager to try them all.

TEXAS BAKLAVA WITH FIGS, PECANS, AND SHERRY-POACHED ASIAN PEARS

From Curt Sassak, The Turtle Restaurant, Brownwood

In the historic town of Brownwood, fourteen miles from the geographic heart of Texas, is a gourmet restaurant dedicated to slow foods and locally sourced ingredients. Mary and David Stanley opened the Turtle Restaurant seven years ago with a mission to feature the products of their neighbors. "It seemed illogical to see animals grazing in nearby fields and still be forced to purchase meat from as far away as New Zealand," says Mary. Their chef de cuisine, Curt Sassak, a native of Washington, D.C., who received his formative training there and abroad, has a similar approach. This is his Texas version of traditional Greek baklava using native figs and pecans with a pear poached in a sherry from McPherson Cellars, one of the oldest vineyards in the state.

FOR THE PEARS:
½ CUP SUGAR
3 CUPS MCPHERSON CELLARS CHANSA SOLERA RESERVA OR ANOTHER GOOD SHERRY
½ TSP ORANGE ZEST
½ TSP LEMON ZEST
3 BOSC OR SECKEL PEARS, PEELED AND CORED FROM THE BOTTOM

FOR THE BAKLAVA:
¾ CUP PLUS 2 TBSP SUGAR
1½ TSP HONEY
½ TSP FRESH LEMON JUICE
¼ CINNAMON STICK
1 WHOLE CLOVE
1 CUP PECANS, FINELY CHOPPED
½ CUP DRIED FIGS, FINELY CHOPPED
½ TSP GROUND CINNAMON
PINCH OF GROUND CLOVES
8 OZ PHYLLO DOUGH, THAWED
1 STICK (8 TBSP) UNSALTED BUTTER, MELTED

Serves 6

POACH THE PEARS:

1 In a saucepan just large enough to contain the upright pears, combine the sugar, sherry, citrus zests, and 1 cup water. Bring the mixture to a boil over medium-high heat; then reduce the heat to a low simmer. Add the pears and cook, covered, until they are soft but not mushy, 15–20 minutes. (To test, insert a metal skewer into a pear. When the skewer goes in with just a little resistance, it is ready.)

2 Remove the pears from the cooking liquid, place on a plate, cover loosely with plastic wrap, and chill.

3 Cook the remaining syrup over medium-high heat until it is reduced to a thick, sticky syrup. Remove from the heat, cover, and reserve at room temperature.

MAKE THE BAKLAVA:

4 To make the syrup, combine ½ cup of the sugar, the honey, lemon juice, cinnamon stick, and whole clove, and 10 tablespoons water in a small saucepan over medium-high heat. Bring to a boil; then reduce the heat to a simmer, cover, and cook for about 5 minutes to dissolve the sugar. Remove the cinnamon stick and clove and let cool.

5 Preheat the oven to 325°F.

6 In a large bowl, combine the remaining sugar and the pecans, figs, ground cinnamon, and ground cloves; set aside.

7 Unroll the phyllo pastry. Lay a 9 x 13-inch baking pan on top of the phyllo and cut the phyllo the same size as the bottom of the pan, using the pan as a stencil. Keep the phyllo covered with a damp towel to prevent it from drying out.

8 Using a pastry brush, brush the bottom and sides of the pan with some of the melted butter. Lay a phyllo sheet on the bottom of the pan, brush with butter, and repeat, using a total of 8 sheets, brushing each sheet with butter. Sprinkle a thin layer of the nut mixture over the top phyllo sheet, just enough to barely cover.

9 Layer 3 more phyllo sheets on top, brushing each with butter, and then sprinkle again with some of the nut mixture. Repeat this process with 3 sheets of phyllo at a time, until the nut mixture is gone. For the top layer, finish with 8 sheets of phyllo.

10 Using a long, very sharp knife, cut the baklava into diamonds. To do this, first cut 4 long rows, and then make 9 diagonal cuts. This should yield 36 diamonds.

11 Pour the remaining butter over the top of the pastry. Bake until evenly golden and flaky, about 1¼ hours.

12 Spoon the cooled baklava syrup over the entire hot pastry. Cool to room temperature. Cut each chilled Asian pear into quarters.

13 To plate, lay out 6 plates, place one piece of baklava with a piece of poached pear on either side and a drizzle of the pear poaching syrup on the plate for a garnish.

MOMMA RAE'S BLACKBERRY BUTTERMILK PIE

From Kate Nelson, Piecurious Catering and Pie Company, Dallas

This pie, featuring Texas blackberries, is a variation of a recipe belonging to Kate Nelson's mother. It also works with fresh blueberries, or a combination of both blueberries and blackberries, a version Nelson calls her "Black and Blue Pie." "I'm using the recipes that have been handed down to me by four generations of amazing women bakers," says Nelson. "A single slice of my mom's pie always puts a smile on my face. My philosophy is that pie solves problems. I hope that each and every Piecurious pie I create will do the same for others—one slice at a time."

Edible Tip

According to Kate Nelson, it's best to use a glass pie plate, especially with this pie. Glass conducts and distributes heat more evenly, making baking times faster and more efficient. The result is a perfect pie every time.

1¾ CUPS SUGAR

3 TBSP FLOUR

3 EGGS AT ROOM TEMPERATURE

1 STICK (8 TBSP) UNSALTED BUTTER, MELTED AND COOLED

1 CUP BUTTERMILK

1½ CUPS FRESH BLACKBERRIES, CRUSHED AND PUSHED THROUGH A FINE-MESH STRAINER

1 (9-INCH) PIE SHELL, FROZEN AND UNBAKED (RECIPE FOLLOWS)

Makes 1 pie

1 Preheat the oven to 350°F.

2 In a large bowl, combine the sugar and flour and whisk to combine. Whisk in the eggs one at a time, blending completely before adding the next one. Blend in the melted butter and buttermilk until the batter is smooth and rather thin. Stir in the strained blackberry pulp until all the darker purple streaks have been well blended.

3 Pour the filling into the chilled pie shell and bake until the surface of the pie puffs and develops small cracks, 45–60 minutes.

4 Cool on a wire rack for several hours. The surface will flatten as it cools, and the small cracks will be less visible. Any leftovers should be stored in the refrigerator, where the slices will keep, covered, up to 5 days.

EDIBLE'S ALL-BUTTER CRUST

Even if you've had disappointing piecrust attempts before, we urge you to give it another shot. We've had feedback from all over the country that this crust, originally published in *Edible Seattle,* works like a charm. It's about the proportion of butter to flour to water—and keeping everything icy cold right up to the point you pop it in the oven.

1¼ CUPS ALL-PURPOSE FLOUR
¼ TSP SALT
1 STICK (8 TBSP) UNSALTED
   BUTTER, CHILLED, CUT
   INTO 1-INCH DICE, AND
   CHILLED AGAIN

UP TO 6 TBSP COLD WATER

Makes 1 generous 9-inch crust

1 Blend the flour and salt in a medium bowl. Sprinkle the chilled butter cubes over the flour and press into the dry ingredients with your fingertips, blending together until the mixture looks like fresh breadcrumbs or damp sand. Ideally, no lumps of butter any bigger than a pea will remain, nor will you have any dry flour lurking in the bottom of the bowl.

2 Add cold water (best chilled in the refrigerator) 1 tablespoon at a time, up to 6 tablespoons, blending gently with a large fork, until the dough forms into a ball.

3 On a lightly floured work surface, roll the dough out to a thickness of ⅛ inch. Transfer it to a 9-inch pie pan and gently fit it in. Trim the edge with a sharp knife or scissors so the dough hangs over the edge by ½ inch. Fold and crimp the dough's edges. Line with plastic wrap and freeze for a minimum of 30 minutes, or as long as overnight.

4 Remove from the freezer when your filling's ready and the oven is preheated—whatever sort of pie you're baking, you want the crust fully frozen when it goes into the oven.

Edible Tips

◆ For a double crust (as used in Uncle Pat's Favorite Poblano Pot Pie, page 43), make 2 batches of dough; roll out and freeze one as directed above. Roll the second batch of dough into a 10-inch circle. Brush off any excess flour, transfer to a parchment paper–lined baking sheet, cover with plastic wrap, and refrigerate until firm, at least 20 minutes.
◆ A pastry cloth is the most helpful piecrust accessory you can have. Lay it out on your rolling surface, cover it heavily with flour, and roll out your crust. Much of the flour will be absorbed by the cloth and the crust will neither stick to the cloth nor absorb so much flour that it dries out. You can find the cloths at kitchen stores and many hardware stores, sold with rolling pin covers. The covers get saggy and aren't worth the trouble, but the pastry cloth itself is a winner.

TEXAS GRAPEFRUIT PIE

From Kate Nelson, Piecurious Catering and Pie Company, Dallas

This pie is reserved for the true blue Texas grapefruit fan, and not for the faint of citrus. The texture is that of a Key lime pie with the appearance of a lemon chess pie. Kate Nelson developed this recipe for the Texas Grapefruit Dinner, hosted by chef Graham Dodds. "He provided me with the best batch of Rio Grande Valley grapefruit that I'd ever seen," says Nelson. "My goal is to create the freshest farm-to-table pie that I can. I always have wonderful luck at Dallas Farmers Market."

Edible Tip

Use the "spoon test" to determine if you have cooked the filling long enough. "This test was passed down to me," says Nelson, "by the long line of matriarchal bakers in my family and has stood the test of time. Before removing the filling mixture from the heat, take a teaspoon and dip out a bit of the filling. Let the spoon rest for about 30 seconds. Spin the spoon upside down and hold it that way. If the filling stays and does not drip or droop down, the filling is finished and is sure to set up properly. If it drips or droops down, boil the filling 5 additional minutes and repeat the test. This trick is extremely useful for all pie fillings that require boiling."

2½ CUPS SUGAR
½ CUP FLOUR
4 EGG YOLKS
4–5 RED MEDIUM GRAPEFRUITS
1 (16 OZ) CAN SWEETENED
  CONDENSED MILK
1 TSP FRESH LEMON JUICE
SEEDS SCRAPED FROM ¼ VANILLA
  BEAN POD OR 1 TSP VANILLA
  EXTRACT

1 (9-INCH) EDIBLE'S ALL-BUTTER
  CRUST (PAGE 133), PREBAKED
  AND COOLED
FRESH WHIPPED CREAM FOR
  GARNISH

Makes 1 (9-inch) pie

1 In a small bowl, whisk together 2 cups of the sugar and the flour; set aside.

2 In a separate small bowl, whisk together the egg yolks; set aside at room temperature.

3 Cut the grapefruit into quarters and remove the fruit from each section of rind, discarding any big pieces of white pith in the center (use clean hands or a paring knife, as you prefer). Place the chunks of peeled fruit in a medium saucepan and add 2 cups water. Slowly bring the mixture to a boil over medium-high heat, stirring constantly. Once the water is boiling, blend in the remaining ½ cup sugar. Boil, stirring frequently, until the fruit is well broken down and the mixture is thick and pulpy, 10–15 minutes.

4 Whisk in the sugar-flour mixture until everything is well blended. Slowly stir in the condensed milk until the mixture is smooth. Pour ½ cup of the hot fruit mixture into the egg yolks and whisk to combine. Pour the tempered egg yolks into the saucepan and blend thoroughly. Stir in the lemon juice. Boil until the mixture is thickened, about 10 minutes. Remove from the heat and stir in the vanilla.

5 Pour the filling into the baked pie shell and refrigerate for at least 2 hours before serving. Top with freshly whipped cream for a grand balance of flavor and texture.

MIMI'S CHOCOLATE CREAM PIE

From Nicole Whittington, home cook, Dallas

A cook's most valuable recipe is often the one passed down from a family elder. For Nicole Whittington, that treasured keepsake is a chocolate pie recipe jotted down by her grandmother Mimi ten years ago on a 4 x 6-inch index card. "I'm so glad I had the presence of mind to ask her for it before she passed away," says Nicole, an avid baker who earned a bakery/pastry degree from El Centro College. "The beauty is in the recipe's simplicity. Its custard thickens easily and sets up well; it's not too heavy, yet it has a richness of flavor and texture." Nicole inherited her grandmother's knack for baking, and her canning skills won her a blue ribbon at the State Fair of Texas. She and her husband, Jeff, a senior producer at KERA-FM, the North Texas public radio station, have a small garden and a brood of backyard chickens at their East Dallas home. Freshly gathered eggs add to the homespun goodness of this chocolaty family recipe passed down with love from grandmother to granddaughter.

2 CUPS WHOLE MILK
¾ CUP SUGAR
⅓ CUP UNBLEACHED ALL-PURPOSE FLOUR
2 TBSP DUTCH PROCESS COCOA
½ TSP SALT
2 LARGE CAGE-FREE EGGS
2 TBSP UNSALTED BUTTER
1 TSP VANILLA EXTRACT
1 (9-INCH) PIE SHELL (PAGE 133), PREBAKED AND COMPLETELY COOLED
FRESH SWEETENED WHIPPED CREAM FOR SERVING

Makes 1 (9-inch) pie

1 Bring the milk, sugar, flour, cocoa, and salt to a simmer in a medium saucepan over medium-high heat, stirring often.

2 In a separate large bowl, whisk the eggs until the whites and yolks are combined.

3 Once the milk mixture begins to simmer, remove from the heat. Slowly whisk 1 cup of the milk mixture, 1–2 tablespoons at a time, into the eggs to temper them.

4 Return the saucepan to the burner. Whisk the tempered eggs into the saucepan and cook over medium heat, stirring constantly, until thickened. (When a spoon is dipped into the mixture, then raised, the mixture should coat the back of the spoon.)

5 Remove the filling from the heat and stir in the butter and vanilla. Pour into the prebaked pie shell and let cool completely for several hours before serving to allow the filling to set up.

6 Top with fresh sweetened whipped cream.

Edible Tip

If you're serving the pie the same day, it is preferable to let it to set up at room temperature. You can also place the pie in the refrigerator to chill and set. Cover it with a clean dish towel or a layer of plastic wrap. This will prevent a crusty film from forming across the top.

FIGGY PIG CANDY

From Beverly Thomas, Cold Springs Farm, Weatherford

Figgy Pig Candy is a southern favorite and a fond memory for Cold Springs Farm's Beverly Thomas, who grew up in rural Mississippi. "My aunt Mabel loved to prepare this with her overripe figs," says Thomas. "She made it with Brer Rabbit syrup, which is still available, in light or full flavor. It's part molasses and part corn syrup, and the full flavor is dark and rich. If you love bacon, you're going to flip over this recipe." At Cold Springs Farm, Thomas uses sustainable farming methods to grow an incredible variety of organic vegetables, fruits, herbs, and flowers, many of which are heirloom or rare to North Texas.

1 PINT OVERRIPE FIGS
1 CUP FULL-FLAVOR BRER RABBIT
  SYRUP
1 LB THICK-CUT BACON
  (ABOUT 12 SLICES)

½ CUP FIRMLY PACKED DARK
  BROWN SUGAR

Makes about 12 candies

1 Preheat the oven to 375°F.

2 Line a baking sheet with foil or parchment paper; then set a wire rack over it (this is to keep the caramelized bacon slices from sticking).

3 Puree the figs in a food processor. Transfer to a medium bowl and stir in the syrup.

4 Dip each slice of bacon in the fig-syrup mixture, and place it on the rack. Sprinkle both sides of each slice with the brown sugar.

5 Bake until the bacon is crisp, about 15 minutes. Let cool and serve.

PEACH AND BLACKBERRY COBBLER

*From Chris Ostlund and
Mark Wooton, Garden Cafe, Dallas*

This down-home dessert is the result of two heavenly pairings: peaches and blackberries, and Larken Farms and the Garden Cafe. Tucked away in old East Dallas, the Garden Cafe, owned by Dale Wootton and his son Mark, is a gathering spot for artists, writers, and a loyal band of locals who love the relaxed setting and the garden-to-table cuisine. Folks can even bring their dogs and linger on the cozy patio near beds of organic herbs and vegetables. Their seasonal cobbler features peaches and blackberries from Larken Farms in Waxahachie. Ken and Laura Jo Halverson grow more than thirty varieties of some of the tastiest peaches and yummiest blackberries in Texas and, like the Woottons, they use organic methods to nurture their seven thousand fruit trees and more than three hundred blackberry bushes. Cinnamon-spiced peaches and blackberries bubbling under a buttery biscuit topping? Oh, my goodness—yes!

3 CUPS ALL-PURPOSE FLOUR
¼ TSP SALT
1½ TBSP BAKING POWDER
2 EGGS
1 CUP WHOLE MILK
2 STICKS (16 TBSP) UNSALTED
  BUTTER, MELTED
1 TSP VANILLA EXTRACT
4 CUPS PITTED, PEELED, AND
  CHOPPED RIPE PEACHES
4 CUPS BLACKBERRIES

JUICE FROM 1 LEMON (ABOUT
  3 TBSP)
½ CUP SUGAR
1 TSP GROUND CINNAMON
DASH OF FRESHLY GRATED NUTMEG
¼ CUP INSTANT TAPIOCA
½ STICK (4 TBSP) CHILLED
  UNSALTED BUTTER

Serves 10

1 Preheat the oven to 350°F. Butter a 9 x 13-inch baking dish.

2 Combine the flour, ⅛ teaspoon of the salt, and the baking powder in large bowl. In a separate bowl, combine the eggs, milk, melted butter, and vanilla and mix well. In a steady stream, stir the liquid ingredients into the dry ingredients. Mix until just combined. Set aside.

3 Put the peach chunks in a large bowl, and carefully fold in the blackberries and lemon juice. In a small bowl, combine the sugar, cinnamon, nutmeg, the remaining ⅛ teaspoon salt, and the tapioca. Sprinkle the sugar-spice mixture over the fruit and gently stir to blend.

4 Pour the fruit mixture into the prepared baking dish. Cut the chilled butter into small chunks and place on top of the fruit. Top the fruit with 10 evenly spaced scoops of the biscuit dough. Then bake until the biscuit topping is golden brown and the filling is bubbling, 25–30 minutes. Serve warm.

BREAD PUDDING WITH TEXAS PECANS
AND LOCAL BOURBON SAUCE

*From Lauren McClure, photojournalist
and frequent contributor to*
Edible Dallas & Fort Worth

This warm, wintery dessert gets its crunch from a food source with ancient roots. Archaeological evidence shows that pecan trees have grown along Texas creek beds and riverbanks for at least five thousand years. To the Native Americans, pecans were a valued resource, nutritious, portable, and easy to preserve after the autumn harvest. Today, Texas is the largest producer of native pecans and second only to Georgia in the production of orchard-grown pecans.

For an added touch of Texas, use locally crafted bourbon when making this recipe. The Garrison Brothers Distillery in the Hill Country produces bourbon made from organic corn grown in the Texas Panhandle. Another option is a distilled spirit from the Balcones Distilling Company in Waco. Though technically not a bourbon, their Balcones Baby Blue, made with roasted Hopi blue corn, works well here. Savor this dessert (and a nip of the spirits) while curled up beside a glowing fire.

FOR THE BREAD PUDDING:
2 CUPS WHOLE MILK
1 CUP HEAVY CREAM
4 CUPS STALE FRENCH BREAD, CUT
    INTO 1-INCH CUBES
2 LARGE EGGS
½ CUP GRANULATED SUGAR
1 TBSP VANILLA EXTRACT
¼ TSP GROUND CINNAMON
¼ TSP NUTMEG
½ STICK (4 TBSP) UNSALTED
    BUTTER, MELTED
⅓ CUP RAISINS

½ CUP PECANS, CHOPPED

FOR THE BOURBON SAUCE:
2 EGG YOLKS
7 TBSP UNSALTED BUTTER
¾ CUP FIRMLY PACKED LIGHT
    BROWN SUGAR
¼ CUP BOURBON

1 TBSP POWDERED SUGAR FOR
SPRINKLING (OPTIONAL)

Serves 6

MAKE THE BREAD PUDDING:

1 Preheat the oven to 350°F.

2 In a large bowl, pour the milk and cream over the cubed bread. Use your hands to evenly coat the cubes and let them soak.

3 In a separate large bowl, beat the eggs together with the sugar until they become a thick, even batter. Add the vanilla, cinnamon, nutmeg, and melted butter and beat for 1 minute. Stir in the raisins and pecans. Add the soaked bread and stir well. Let stand for at least 20 minutes.

4 Transfer the mixture to a baking dish (1⅛-quart oval or 1¾-quart rectangle). Bake until firm in the center and the top is golden brown, about 45 minutes.

MAKE THE BOURBON SAUCE:

5 In a small bowl, beat the egg yolks until they are thick and uniform in color.

6 In a small saucepan, melt the butter with brown sugar. Stir well and cook until the sugar melts and loses its grain. Remove from the heat, let cool slightly, and then pour the butter-sugar mixture over the egg yolks a little at a time and beat together until thickened. Stir in the bourbon. Set aside and keep warm.

7 To serve, pour spoonfuls of the warm sauce over each plated serving. Sprinkle with powdered sugar, if desired.

STRAWBERRIES WITH ROMANOFF SAUCE

From Kelly Yandell,
TheMeaningofPie.com

Texas strawberries are a bright but fleeting springtime treat. They thrive in the short and temperamental period before the real heat sets in, though a few talented gardeners have been known to cultivate plump and beautiful strawberries well into the hot days. Strawberries are members of the rose family, along with apples, pears, raspberries, and other unexpected cousins. They're full of vitamin C, they're delicious, and they're a guaranteed hit with kids and adults alike. This preparation comes from Kelly Yandell, the Dallas-based force behind the blog *The Meaning of Pie,* and is simple and fast and produces a dessert that is both refined and basic—a taste of spring and a bit of decadence.

FOR THE STRAWBERRIES:

1 LB STRAWBERRIES, HULLED AND
    QUARTERED
1 TBSP GRANULATED SUGAR
1 TBSP COINTREAU OR OTHER
    ORANGE LIQUEUR

FOR THE SAUCE:

½ CUP WHIPPING CREAM
3 TBSP LIGHT BROWN SUGAR
½ CUP SOUR CREAM
1 TSP VANILLA EXTRACT
SEEDS SCRAPED FROM HALF OF A
    VANILLA BEAN POD

Serves 4

PREPARE THE STRAWBERRIES:

1 Place the quartered strawberries in a bowl and sprinkle them with the granulated sugar and Cointreau. Mix gently with a spoon so that the sugar and alcohol are well distributed. Cover the bowl with plastic wrap and refrigerate for at least 20 minutes and up to 4 hours.

MAKE THE SAUCE:

2 In a chilled metal bowl, begin whipping the cream with either a whisk or an electric mixer. Once the cream just begins to thicken, sprinkle in 2 teaspoons of the brown sugar and whip until the sugar has been incorporated. Continue whipping the cream and adding sugar in small batches until all the sugar is incorporated and the cream has formed stiff peaks. With a broad silicone spatula, fold in the sour cream, vanilla extract, and vanilla seeds. Refrigerate until you are ready to serve.

3 Serve each guest a bowl of the strawberries with a big dollop of the sauce on top.

Edible Tips

♦ This recipe is a luscious substitute for strawberry shortcake, if it's too hot for baking shortcakes or if you'll be serving gluten-sensitive friends or family.
♦ To obtain vanilla seeds, slice a vanilla pod lengthwise down the center. Peel it open and use the back of a knife to scrape out the thousands of black specks, which are the seeds. Put the scraped vanilla pod in a small jar of granulated sugar. In a few days, you will have a delicious and fragrant vanilla sugar. If you prefer, you can skip the vanilla beans and add an additional ½ teaspoon vanilla extract to the sauce.

LEMON HONEY CAKE

From Graham Dodds, Hotel Palomar, formerly with Bolsa, Dallas

Graham Dodds learned to appreciate bees and bountiful kitchen gardens during childhood visits to his grandparents' house in England. In a small coastal town located on the border of England and Scotland, his grandfather maintained ten hives and his grandmother had a thriving garden. His grandfather's raw, untreated honey is a memory that's distinct. "It changed with the seasons," says Dodds, "depending on what wildflowers were in bloom." Today he maintains several hives of his own in Dallas and Waxahachie and features honey in many of his recipes, including his signature Lemon Honey Cake. One of his favorite local honeys is the Texas Honeybee Guild's Zip Code Honey, which can be purchased at Bolsa Mercado, a fresh foods market in the Bishop Arts District of Dallas.

COOKING SPRAY
¼ CUP PLUS 1 TBSP GRANULATED SUGAR
1½ CUPS BREAD FLOUR
½ CUP SLIVERED BLANCHED ALMONDS
1½ TSP BAKING POWDER
4 LARGE EGGS
½ CUP HONEY

ZEST AND JUICE OF 2 LEMONS
¼ CUP WHOLE MILK
1 STICK (8 TBSP) UNSALTED BUTTER, MELTED
1 CUP FRESH BERRIES AND FRESH WHIPPED CREAM FOR GARNISH

Serves 8

1 Preheat the oven to 350°F. Lightly coat a 10-inch round cake pan with cooking spray and dust with 1 tablespoon granulated sugar, tapping out the excess. Make sure the pan is evenly coated.

2 Combine the remaining ¼ cup sugar and the flour, almonds, and baking powder in a food processor. Pulse until the almond slivers are pulverized; set aside.

3 Combine the eggs, honey, and lemon zest in the bowl of a stand mixer and beat, using the paddle attachment, on medium-high until the mixture is pale yellow in color and has a ribbony consistency, about 2 minutes. Using a silicone spatula, gently fold the lemon juice and milk into the egg mixture. Next, gently fold in the flour mixture, being careful to just incorporate the flour. (The cake will be tough if the flour is overworked.) Gently fold in the melted butter.

4 Pour the batter into the prepared cake pan and bake until the top is light brown and a toothpick inserted comes out clean, about 20 minutes. Serve warm with fresh berries and whipped cream.

Edible Tips

♦ When using a traditional zester, be sure you remove just the yellow part—the zest. Don't use the white pith just beneath—it's bitter.
♦ At the ribbon stage, an egg mixture is stiff enough to form ribbons as it drops back into the bowl from a raised beater, spoon, or whisk.
♦ Dodds suggests serving this cake with a chunk of honeycomb to accent the honey in the cake.

HONEY FLAN

From Cosme Alcantar, Blue Mesa Grill, five locations in the Dallas & Fort Worth Metroplex

Blue Mesa Grill has been serving this traditional Mexican egg custard since they first opened their doors, and it is still one of their most popular desserts at all their locations. Baked in individual custard cups, the flan is inverted when served and the excess soft caramel is used as a sauce. These are nice garnished with berries in season.

1 QT PLUS 1 CUP HEAVY WHIPPING CREAM

1 TBSP VANILLA EXTRACT

1 CINNAMON STICK

7 EGGS

1 CUP PLUS 2 TBSP HONEY

1 CUP PLUS 2 TBSP SUGAR

Serves 10

1 Preheat the oven to 350°F.

2 Combine the cream, vanilla, and cinnamon stick in a medium saucepan and bring to a gentle boil without scorching. Remove from the heat.

3 While the cream is heating, whisk the eggs, honey, and ½ cup of the sugar together in a large bowl until smooth.

4 Combine the cream and egg mixture and whip vigorously together. Strain through a fine-mesh strainer.

5 Heat the remaining ½ cup plus 2 tablespoons sugar in a small sauté pan over medium heat, stirring continuously until a rich-colored caramel is formed.

6 Place 10 straight-sided, ceramic soufflé cups in a large roasting pan. As soon as the sugar syrup is ready, divide it equally among the 10 cups.

7 Divide the cream mixture among the caramel-lined cups to just below the rim.

8 Pour enough hot water into the roasting pan to come three-quarters of the way up the sides of cups. Bake the flans until set in the center, 45–50 minutes.

9 Cool, cover, and refrigerate at least 4 hours and up to 2 days.

10 Run small knife around the custards to loosen. To unmold, place a small plate atop each custard; firmly holding the plate and custard cup together, invert, and shake gently, allowing the custard and caramel to settle onto the plate.

FARM-FRESH BLUEBERRIES AND MELON WITH FETA

From Cathy Barber, Food Editor, the
Dallas Morning News

Think of Texas blueberries as a gateway food. Picking berries is a fabulous way to introduce little ones to the experience of acquiring fresh, local fruits and vegetables. Blueberries are a relatively recent addition to the Texas landscape, with Texas A&M University taking the lead in the early 1980s helping establish the industry with the Texas-tough blueberry: Rabbiteye. Today East Texas is dotted with farms, including many that will let you pick your own; for a couple of dollars more, they'll do the picking for you. Many have a farm stand where pickers can stock up on local jams and preserves and other produce too. This dish is simple, but it's Cathy Barber's favorite way to enjoy fresh blueberries.

Edible Tips

• This dish is especially lovely when made with the more unusual yellow-flesh watermelon.
• Rabbiteye blueberries (*Vaccinium ashei*) are very common all over the American South and are available at any good farmers' market. Buy the plants at local nurseries everywhere.

2 PINTS BLUEBERRIES, RINSED
4 CUPS CUBED WATERMELON
4 OZ FETA CHEESE, OR TO TASTE, CRUMBLED

2 TSP CHOPPED FRESH MINT (OPTIONAL)

Serves 4

1 In a large bowl, gently combine the blueberries and cubed watermelon.

2 Sprinkle on the crumbled feta, garnish with the mint, and serve immediately.

KATHERINE CLAPNER

Dude, Sweet Chocolate, Dallas

The vibe on the tree-lined streets of Dallas's Bishop Arts District is both hip and old school: artsy murals on vintage buildings, an Americana soda shop, and a bike store beside trendy restaurants. Around the corner, Katherine Clapner is forever reimagining chocolates and other confections at her Dude, Sweet Chocolate shop.

Don't be fooled by her impish good looks and casual demeanor. Clapner has impressive credentials and takes her sweets quite seriously. The Arlington, Texas, native received her formal education at the Culinary Institute of America in Hyde Park, New York, and spent her formative years at the Savoy Hotel in London, the Four Seasons and Charlie Trotter's in Chicago, and the Windsor Court in New Orleans. But she credits the ten years she worked with iconic Texas chef Stephan Pyles as being the most influential.

"Stephan taught me to keep evolving," says Clapner. "I'm always looking for new ways to do the ordinary. You'll never see me making the usual chocolate-dipped strawberry."

Her latest invention, the M'Tini Truffle, blends Guittard chocolate with vodka, violets, and lime. Her chocolates are all dark and evocative of locales near and far. Recent more savory inventions include Parique, flavored with Louisiana tobacco and cognac, and Black Gold, mixing black garlic and sweet wild mushrooms. For her sweet chocolates, she has combined Texas cabernet with golden raisins, passion fruit and ginger salt, fresh lemon with buttermilk, and rose petal jam and marzipan. Even the

words pique the senses. Her combinations may sometimes seem unusual, but they're never boring.

"The goal in all the things that I make," she says, "is to create a taste that's familiar, but not overwhelming or obvious. It's all about balance."

Clapner is partial to local ingredients and adamant about supporting other regional food artisans. Her Hill Country chocolates are made with local Zip Code honey and the Dallas Mozzarella Company's goat crema. She also uses dairy products from Lucky Layla Farms in suburban Plano and beer from Rahr & Sons Brewing Company in Fort Worth and Franconia Brewing Company in McKinney.

Besides chocolates, Clapner also creates gourmet sorbets and frozen yogurts in individual to-go tubs, a favorite of Bishop Arts strollers.

"I live within a block of the Dallas Farmers Market, and just bought a giant box of peaches from Mr. Lemley. I also get lots of fresh fruit from Tom Spicer at FM 1410. I don't want to be put in a corner. If there's a day when Tom has a load of citrus, then that's what I'm using. I can take something that's slightly bruised, and it's still perfect for my needs. These are the freshest fruits in Dallas."

In the summer, her dreamy frozen concoctions mix local blueberries and crème, blackberries and coconut oolong, and hickory-smoked peach with white chocolate.

Clapner is determined to continue growing as a chef. "It would be myopic and boring to always keep doing the same thing," she continues. "Stephan taught me that. He opened my eyes to what it means to be a chef."

TURKISH COFFEE TRUFFLES

From Katherine Clapner,
Dude, Sweet Chocolate, Dallas

In the heart of Dallas's Bishop Arts District, confectioner Katherine Clapner whips up an ever-changing assortment of artisanal chocolates. Her menu reads like a travelogue. Some creations at the Dude, Sweet Chocolate shop conjure up the images of far-flung locales like a Tahitian beach or a market in Marrakech. Other morsels are nostalgic reminders of memories closer to home: a Texas lavender field or Grandma's kitchen. Clapner sources her milk, honey, herbs, and fruits locally. "If you've got a great dairy resource right down the road, you'd be crazy not to use it," she says. "You can really taste the difference." In her exotic Turkish Coffee Truffles, she uses fresh cream from Lucky Layla Farms and local honey from the hives of the Texas Honeybee Guild. Each chocolate mouthful blends the dark hues of Turkish coffee with the bright flavors of flower water and tahini.

Edible Tips

* Other nut butters or even table butter can replace tahini.
* Whiskey can be used to replace flower water and cane syrup can replace honey.
* Any finely ground coffee of choice can replace the Turkish coffee.

FOR THE TRUFFLES:
12 OZ DARK CHOCOLATE (65% CACAO OR HIGHER), ROUGHLY CHOPPED
¾ CUP PLUS 2 TBSP HEAVY CREAM
½ CUP LOCAL HONEY
2 TBSP FINELY GROUND TURKISH COFFEE (DRY GRANULES)
FINELY GRATED ZEST OF ¼ ORANGE
2 TBSP TAHINI (SESAME BUTTER), AT ROOM TEMPERATURE
¾ TSP SEA SALT
1 TBSP ORANGE BLOSSOM WATER OR 1½ TSP ROSE WATER

FOR THE COATING:
8 OZ DARK CHOCOLATE (65% CACAO OR HIGHER), ROUGHLY CHOPPED
½ CUP POWDERED SUGAR, OR ¾ CUP DUTCH PROCESS COCOA POWDER, OR 1½ CUPS FINELY GROUND NUTS

Makes 24 (1½-inch) balls

1 In a heavy saucepan or double boiler set over low heat, carefully melt the chocolate, stirring until it is smooth; set aside.

2 In another saucepan, heat the cream, honey, coffee, and orange zest to just under a boil. (Be careful not to let the mixture boil.) Remove from the burner and let set for 5 minutes.

3 Strain the cream mixture through a fine-mesh sieve; then whisk into the melted chocolate. Let the mixture come to room temperature. Whisk in the tahini until the mixture completely smooth and shiny. Stir in the salt and orange water. Cover and refrigerate overnight.

4 The next day, roll the chilled mixture into 1½-inch balls. Refrigerate until you are ready to coat.

5 Melt the chocolate for the coating in the top of a double boiler over simmering water, stirring until smooth. Set aside to cool.

6 When the melted chocolate is cool, roll the truffle balls in it, and then toss them in your choice of powered sugar, cocoa, ground nuts, or a combination of two or three.

PERSIMMON BELLINIS

From Tom Motley, Tom Motley North Texas Gardens, McKinney

Native Texas persimmons are an acquired taste. As a kid Tom Motley ate them fresh from his grandmother's tree, a local species commonly known as a possumwood, which bore fruit not much bigger than a Ping-Pong ball. "If there was an early hard freeze, the persimmons were soft and sweet," says Motley, "but they could also be so astringent that your mouth would be puckered for hours." Today, Motley prefers Japanese varieties, which are much larger. His preference is the Tamopan, which grows well in Northeast Texas. It bears a unique squat fruit: its upper half appears to be constricted, as if bound by a too-tight belt. If you're fortunate enough to obtain native persimmons that are fresh but still astringent, place them inside a plastic bag and freeze them overnight to mimic their natural hard-frost ripening.

3 OR 4 VERY RIPE FUYU, TAMOPAN, OR HACHIYA PERSIMMONS
1 CUP ICE CUBES
½ CUP FRESH-SQUEEZED ORANGE JUICE, STRAINED (NO PULP)
2 JIGGERS PEACH BRANDY

1 (750 ML) BOTTLE CHILLED CHAMPAGNE, PROSECCO, OR ANY SPARKLING WINE
12 STRAWBERRIES FOR GARNISH (OPTIONAL)

Makes 12 cocktails

1 Slice open the persimmons, scoop out their flesh, place it in a blender, and puree until smooth. Add half the ice cubes and continue to puree until any large chunks of ice are gone and the mixture is thick and slushy. Add the orange juice, peach brandy, and remaining ice and continue to puree until smooth.

2 Into a Champagne flute, pour 1 ounce of the persimmon slush and top with 2 ounces Champagne.

3 Serve immediately, with a split strawberry on the rim as a garnish, if you like.

Edible Tip

The sweetness of the Bellini can be altered by your choice of sparkling wine. Tom Motley suggests Prosecco Brut as the perfect vehicle to balance the hearty persimmon puree.

THE SUMMER GARDEN

From Paula Angerstein,
Paula's Texas Spirits, Austin

What do you do when there are more cucumbers and basil in your garden than you know what to do with? How about a seasonal drink? Also in the shaker is Paula's Texas Lemon, a limoncello-type liqueur handcrafted in Austin. To show off another Texas product, we've paired it with Dripping Springs Vodka.

1 (1-INCH-THICK) SLICE CUCUMBER, ROUGHLY CHOPPED
4 LARGE FRESH BASIL LEAVES
2 OZ PAULA'S TEXAS LEMON OR OTHER LIMONCELLO
1 OZ VODKA (DRIPPING SPRINGS PREFERRED)
½ OZ FRESH LEMON JUICE
FRESH BASIL SPRIG FOR GARNISH

Makes 1 serving

1 Muddle the cucumber, basil, and Paula's Texas Lemon in a shaker glass.

2 Add the vodka and lemon juice. Shake with ice and double strain into a cocktail glass filled with crushed ice. Garnish with the basil sprig.

FIRE AND BRIMSTONE

From Brian McCullough, Standard
Pour, Dallas

Balcones Distilling of Waco uses Texas scrub oak to imbue its Brimstone Corn Whisky with the smoky aromas of a Texas campfire. Named one of GQ's Most Inspired bartenders in 2011, Brian McCullough recently opened Standard Pour in Dallas. Having worked most of his career at bars that promote local and freshly grown ingredients, all of McCullough's cocktails reflect that philosophy.

Edible Tip

The flamed orange peel adds a bit of citrus flavor to the drink, but you can omit it, if you'd like. Use caution. Liquor is highly flammable, so keep the flame away from your drink.

2 OZ BALCONES BRIMSTONE WHISKY, A TEXAS SCRUB OAK-SMOKED CORN WHISKY
¾ OZ ORANGE/CINNAMON TEA-INFUSED SWEET VERMOUTH
¾ OZ BENEDICTINE
3 DASHES ROOT BEER BITTERS
ABSINTHE RINSE
FLAMED TEXAS ORANGE PEEL

Makes one drink

1 Add whiskey, vermouth, Benedictine, and bitters into a mixing glass and stir for 20 seconds. In a separate Old Fashioned glass, rinse with absinthe and discard. Add one large ice cube into Old Fashioned glass, then strain cocktail into glass. Carefully use a match to flame and caramelize a strip of orange zest (there will be a quick burst of flame as the heat briefly ignites the peel). Rub zest over rim of glass, then drop into drink.

ORANGE/CINNAMON TEA-INFUSED SWEET VERMOUTH:
Place 4 tablespoons of loose-leaf orange/cinnamon tea in lidded jar with 1½ cups of sweet vermouth. Cover and refrigerate for 24 hours. Strain out loose tea and return to jar.

LAVENDER-MINT GIMLET

From Bill Norris, for Dripping Springs Vodka, Dripping Springs

Celebrate Texas's lavender growers with this floral- and mint-scented cocktail featuring Texas's own Dripping Springs Vodka. The Texas Lavender Association was founded in 2008 to promote this growing industry. In the Texas Hill Country, there's a Lavender Trail and a Lavender Festival in the town of Blanco. In North Texas, June Hand is living out a lifelong dream growing lavender at her Purple Ranch Lavender Farm in Royse City. Her fragrant lavender products known for their soothing properties are in high demand at area farmers' markets.

The Kelleher family handcrafts their vodka in the little town of Drippings Springs outside of Austin, using mineral-rich artesian springwater. According to legend, master distiller Gary Kelleher's great-great-grandfather was a vodka maker for the czar of Russia.

1½ OZ VODKA, PREFERABLY DRIPPING SPRINGS
1 OZ (2 TBSP) FRESH LIME JUICE
1 OZ (2 TBSP) LAVENDER-MINT SYRUP (RECIPE FOLLOWS)

LIME SLICE OR FRESH MINT SPRIG FOR GARNISH (OPTIONAL)

Serves 1

1 Combine the vodka, lime juice, and lavender-mint syrup with ice in a cocktail shaker, shake, and strain into a chilled martini glass. Garnish with a lime wheel or a sprig of fresh mint if you like.

LAVENDER-MINT SYRUP

Edible Tip

Dried culinary lavender flowers are available in many grocery stores in the bulk tea section.

1 CUP SUGAR
½ CUP LOOSELY PACKED FRESH MINT LEAVES

½ TSP DRIED LAVENDER FLOWERS

Makes about 2½ cups

1 In a small saucepan, bring the sugar, mint, lavender flowers, and 1 cup water to a low boil over medium heat. Cover, reduce the heat to low, and simmer for 10 minutes.

2 Remove from the heat, uncover, let cool to room temperature, and strain the syrup through a fine-mesh strainer. Store in an airtight jar in the refrigerator for up to 3 weeks.

PAT BRENNAN

Brennan Vineyards, Comanche

Texas vineyard owner Pat Brennan believes Viognier will soon become known as the white wine of Texas. At Brennan Vineyards in Comanche, it is his signature wine, and there are other Texas producers—McPherson Cellars, Becker Vineyards, Grape Creek Vineyards, among others—that are creating Viogniers worthy of notice.

"We describe it as a white wine for red wine lovers," says Brennan. "It has a thick mouthfeel, and it's aromatic with the scents of peach, apricot, and honey."

Sommelier Hunter Hammett, wine director at the Fairmont Dallas hotel, agrees: "Viognier and Texas, in both the culinary and viticulture aspects, are right for each other. The grape is an excellent partner for spicy and creamy foods due to its fruit-first and full-bodied nature. These vines require a relatively warm climate and are thankfully drought resistant."

Hammett was introduced to Brennan's Viognier several years ago when judging a regional competition. "I was so impressed with the quality and character of it that I requested the name of the producer after the judging was complete," says Hammett. "I was ecstatic that it was not only from Texas but from Comanche. It has been

a staple on my wine list ever since."

Brennan Vineyard's rising profile parallels that of the entire Texas wine industry, which in the last decade has been rapidly expanding and receiving increasingly good reviews. In 2001, there were only 46 vineyards in the state. By the beginning of 2011, that number had jumped to 220.

In 1997, with no thought of becoming winemakers, Pat Brennan, then

a practicing physician, and his wife, Trellise, purchased a historic 1879 limestone cottage in the little town of Comanche, two hours southwest of their home in Fort Worth. Located in the Cross Timbers region of Central Texas, Comanche sits at the junction of two of the state's best-known wine regions: the Hill Country and the High Plains.

"It was a place to get away," says Brennan. "Then one thing led to another. Thirty adjacent acres were available on Indian Creek, and we bought it. A

friend, Dr. Richard Becker, has a successful winery in Fredericksburg, and his story is much the same. There was extra property and he decided 'Why not?' We tested our soil and water. It looked good, so Trellise and I bought a tractor and began clearing."

They gathered friends and family and planted fifty-four hundred vines—Viognier, Cabernet, and Syrah—in four days. The intention was to sell grapes to other winemakers, but the quality of their 2003 and 2004 harvests was so good, they soon decided to take the plunge and create their own wines. Today Brennan and his winemaker, Todd Webster, produce eleven varieties.

Recently, Brennan wrote a piece for the Tarrant County Medical Society entitled "Combining Art and Science Outside of Medicine." Statistics show that physicians compared to other professionals are involved in the wine industry in proportionally high numbers.

"Doctors aren't intimidated by chemistry, which is a big part of making a great wine," says Brennan. "But like practicing medicine, winemaking is both a science and an art. You can measure it every step of the way, but ultimately you have to ask, 'How does it taste, look, smell?' That's when it becomes art."

TREATY OAK RUM APPLE CIDER

From Jordan Swim, Vestals Foods and Food Creates Community, Dallas

Served in warmed mugs, this steaming apple cider, spiced with cinnamon, ginger, and dark agave, will warm the coldest night. Created by Jordan Swim of Vestals Foods, it is a winter soother laced with two Texas favorites: Treaty Oak rum and grapefruit juice. The official fruit of Texas, the red grapefruit was first planted in the Rio Grande Valley nearly one hundred years ago. Experts agree that it is among the sweetest in the world. Jordan Swim has traveled all over the world, but he learned the art of entertaining from his parents, and from his grandparents, who always had a flourishing kitchen garden, he learned the lesson of seasonal eating. Though he teaches culinary arts at Allen High School and owns a catering company, three years ago, he and his wife, Emily, decided to begin Food Creates Community, an ongoing series of pop-up dinners featuring seasonal, local foods.

4 CUPS UNFILTERED ORGANIC
 APPLE CIDER
2 CINNAMON STICKS, BROKEN
6 WHOLE CLOVES
1 TBSP DICED FRESH GINGER
¼ CUP FRESH GRAPEFRUIT PULP,
 SEEDS REMOVED
1 TBSP GRAPEFRUIT ZEST

1 TBSP DARK AGAVE SYRUP
4 OZ SHOTS RUM (TREATY OAK
 PLATINUM RUM PREFERRED)
THIN APPLE SLICES AND FRESHLY
 GRATED NUTMEG FOR GARNISH
 (OPTIONAL)

Serves 4

1 Combine the cider, cinnamon sticks, cloves, ginger, and grapefruit pulp and zest in a medium saucepan over medium-low heat and simmer, covered, for 20 minutes.

2 Warm 4 (10-ounce) mugs with warm water. Strain the mulled cider into a pitcher through a fine-mesh strainer and blend in the agave syrup and rum. Divide evenly among the warm mugs and garnish each with an apple slice and a grating of fresh nutmeg, if you like.

BLACK AND BLUE LEMONADE

*From Eva Greer, The Greer Farm,
Daingerfield*

Troubles melt away when you're sitting in a rocker on Sid and Eva Greer's broad wraparound porch with a glass of black and blue lemonade in hand. Above the double screen doors leading into the farmhouse, a sign reads "All Because Two People Fell in Love." Greer Farm is a unique rural haven located near the East Texas town of Daingerfield. Starting in early summer, you can come and pick your own blueberries, blackberries, figs, and plums. Rent one of the four log cabins nestled beside their spring-fed lake, and take one of chef Eva Greer's cooking classes, utilizing the season's harvest. This beautiful berry-infused lemonade is one of Eva's signature summer drinks.

2 CUPS SUGAR
ZEST AND JUICE OF 8 LEMONS
   (ABOUT 1½ CUPS JUICE)
1 CUP BLACKBERRIES

1 CUP BLUEBERRIES
EXTRA BERRIES AND LEMON
   WEDGES FOR GARNISH

Serves 4

1 Bring 2 cups water and the sugar to a boil in a small saucepan. Stir until the sugar is completely dissolved, about 30 seconds, and turn off the heat. Let cool to room temperature.

2 In a large pitcher, combine the sugar syrup, lemon zest and juice, and another 2 cups water; stir until well blended.

3 Combine the berries in a blender and blend until pulverized. Strain through a fine-mesh strainer to remove the seeds. Stir the juice into the lemonade pitcher. Chill thoroughly before serving, or serve with extra ice. Garnish with a few whole berries (float them in the drink) and a lemon wedge.

THE BONNIE AND CLYDE

THE BONNIE AND CLYDE

From Eddie "Lucky" Campbell, The Chesterfield, formerly at Bolsa, Dallas

It's sunset, a Thursday, and happy hour is in full swing. With a fedora on his head and sweat on his brow, bartender Eddie "Lucky" Campbell wields a shaker in each hand, rocking the cocktails with all the ferocity of a zealous maraca player. He pulls in multiple drink orders from his regulars without skipping a beat and tries to strike the perfect balance between speedy delivery and attention to quality; after all, this is a guy who refers to certain mint leaves as having "good character." In this gin-based beverage, the sage imparts a brawny vigor while the house-made Texas plum jelly lends a silken, almost effervescent caress.

1 HEAPING TBSP PLUM JELLY
1½ OZ HAYMAN'S OLD TOM GIN
6 FRESH SAGE LEAVES
½ OZ ST-GERMAIN ELDERFLOWER
    LIQUEUR
½ OZ FRESH LEMON JUICE
LIME WEDGE AND SPRIG FRESH
    SAGE FOR GARNISH (OPTIONAL)

Serves 1

1 Combine the jelly, gin, sage, elderflower liqueur, and lemon juice in a shaker filled with ice and shake vigorously.

2 Strain into a stemmed glass and garnish with a lime wedge and sprig of sage, if you like.

TEXAS TWO-STEP SIPPER

From Hunter Hammett, Pyramid Restaurant & Bar, Fairmont, Dallas

Peach tea is best when sipped from an ice-cold Mason jar, according to Hunter Hammett, the WSET® (Wine & Spirit Education Trust) Advanced Certified sommelier of the Fairmont hotel's Pyramid Restaurant & Bar. For local honey and fresh mint, Hammett heads to the hotel's terrace, where the bees of the Texas Honey Bee Guild thrive in a three-thousand-square-foot garden.

HALF OF A RIPE TEXAS PEACH,
    PEELED, PITTED, AND CUT INTO
    SLICES
3 MINT LEAVES
½ OZ FRESH LEMON JUICE
2 OZ VODKA, PREFERABLY
    DRIPPING SPRINGS OR TITO'S
2 DASHES PEACH BITTERS,
    PREFERABLY FEE BROTHERS
½ OZ LOCAL HONEY
5 OZ COLD-PRESSED BLACK TEA
3 OZ CLUB SODA
MINT SPRIG FOR GARNISH

Makes one drink

1 Drop peach slices, mint leaves, lemon juice, vodka, bitters, and honey into a Mason jar (or a 12 ounce glass) and lightly muddle ingredients until honey dissolves.

2 Add tea and club soda, fill glass with ice, and stir. Garnish with fresh mint sprig, if desired.

MICHAEL'S EASY BREEZY FROZEN MOJITOS

*From Michael Fladmark
and Jean Bothe,
Environmental Activists, Tool*

On a lovely late spring afternoon, four *Edible Dallas & Fort Worth* taste testers spent some quality time on Michael Fladmark and Jean Bothe's East Texas porch sampling local rums while admiring the couple's thriving gardens and beehive. Michael made us his mojitos in two batches: first, with Treaty Oak Platinum Rum from Austin, and then with Railean Texas White Rum from the Galveston area. For each, he muddled fresh mint from his garden, popped open a fizzy bottle of Topo Chico sparkling water, and then came the shortcut—a can of frozen limeade. After several hours swinging on the porch swing, sipping mojitos, the testers unanimously agreed that both Texas rums were polished and flavorful and that, sometimes, shortcuts were okay.

1 (6 OZ) CAN FROZEN LIMEADE
6 OZ WHITE RUM
1–2 CUPS CRUSHED ICE
18–20 FRESH MINT LEAVES
6–10 OZ SPARKLING WATER

4 SPRIGS FRESH MINT AND
4 LIME WEDGES FOR GARNISH
(OPTIONAL)

Serves 4

1 Pour the can of frozen limeade, the rum (use the empty limeade can to measure it), and 1 cup of crushed ice into a blender.

2 Place the mint in a small bowl. Using a muddler or the back of a spoon, gently mash the leaves until they are bruised and have released their minty essence.

3 Add the muddled mint and sparkling water (again, use the limeade can to measure it) into the blender. Blend, adding more ice and more sparkling water as necessary to create a thick, smooth, frozen slush.

4 Serve in wide-mouthed margarita glasses, garnished with a sprig of mint and a wedge of lime if you like.

Edible Tip

You can replace the frozen limeade with 3 ounces of simple syrup and the juice of 3 medium limes (about 3 ounces). To make simple syrup: combine equal amounts of sugar and water in a saucepan over medium-high heat and bring to a boil, stirring constantly to dissolve the sugar. Turn the heat to low and cook briefly, until the syrup is clear and the sugar is entirely dissolved. Let cool before pouring into a clean, tightly sealed jar. Store in the refrigerator for up to 1 month.

These are but a few of the many fine farms, ranches, and food artisans located in our region.

BEVERAGES

BRENNAN VINEYARDS, COMANCHE
Located on the Way Out Wineries wine trail, Brennan Vineyards is one of Texas's 200 wineries. Enthusiasts can travel a dozen wine trails and meet winemakers like Dr. Pat Brennan. Texas is the fifth-largest wine-producing state in the nation. Its emerging signature grapes include Tempranillo, Sangiovese, Grenache, Viognier, and Vermentino. *BrennanVineyards.com; GoTexanWine.org*

FRANCONIA BREWING COMPANY, MCKINNEY
Bavarian native Dennis Wehrmann, who descends from a long line of German brewers, founded Franconia in 2008. Franconia beers can be found in your favorite area restaurants and taverns. Their facilities are state-of-the-art in energy efficiency, and they recycle their mash to feed local cattle. Tours are every Saturday at 11 a.m. *FranconiaBrewing.com*

RAHR & SONS BREWING, FORT WORTH
North Texas brewing pioneer Fritz Rahr opened his Fort Worth operation in 2004, tagging it "the new brewery with the 150-year history." It all began with his great-great-grandfather, a German immigrant, who opened his Wisconsin brewery in 1847. Rahr beers can be found in neighborhood pubs and local grocery stores. Their popular brewery tours are offered on Wednesdays and Sundays. *RahrBrewing.com*

BREAD AND GRAINS

EMPIRE BAKING, DALLAS
Artisan bakers Robert and Meaders Ozarow use purified water, King Arthur flour, natural sea salt, and other quality ingredients for their handcrafted breads and baked goods. *EmpireBaking.com*

GRAPEVINE GRAINS, GRAPEVINE
Steve and Vickie Smolek specialize in freshly milled stone-ground flour and freshly rolled oats. Their product line also includes granolas, muesli, and Texas trail mix. *GrapevineGrains.com*

HOMESTEAD HERITAGE GRITS, ELM MOTT
A centerpiece of the Brazos de Dios sustainable farming community is their historic water-powered, timber-frame mill (circa 1760). Grains processed here include fourteen types of organically grown corn, wheat, rye, and oats. Homestead grits—white, yellow, or blue—are used by a number of local chefs. *HomesteadGristmill.com*

CHEESE

BRAZOS VALLEY CHEESE, ELM MOTT
Marc Kuehl and Rebeccah Durkin use raw Jersey cow's milk and natural ingredients to make their award-winning cheeses. Smoked varieties are laid over pecan shells in a restored 1860s smokehouse. Marc and Rebeccah are part of the thousand-member Brazos de Dios religious community. *BrazosValleyCheese.com*

ROOFTOP GARDEN AT THE FAIRMONT DALLAS HOTEL

CAPRINO ROYALE, WACO
Eric Tippit and Karen Dierolf's purebred herd of Nubian goats produce high-quality milk known for its rich butterfat content. Their luscious Texas Bloombonnet, a soft mold-ripened goat cheese, is a favorite among cheese connoisseurs. *CaprinoRoyale.com*

EAGLE MOUNTAIN CHEESE, GRANBURY
Dave Eagle and his son Matt are relatively new to the cheese-making business, but their Birdsville Reserve has already garnered a national award. Their Goudas are made of fresh raw milk from Brown Swiss cows, naturally raised in North Texas. *EagleMountainCheese.com*

MOZZARELLA COMPANY, DALLAS
Celebrating its thirtieth birthday in 2012, the Mozzarella Company is the grand dame of artisanal cheese producers in Texas. Entrepreneur Paula Lambert and her cadre of mostly women cheese makers handcraft fresh mozzarella and over twenty other varieties of cow's milk and goat's milk cheeses from age-old recipes. *MozzCo.com*

ON PURE GROUND DAIRY, BONHAM
Cheryl and Paul Haubrich's dairy is located on fifty-two pristine acres near Bonham. Their chèvre, crafted in small batches in the French tradition, is light and elegant; some have minced bit of figs, peaches, apricots, and other delights. *OnPureGround.com*

VELDHUIZEN TEXAS FARMSTEAD CHEESE, DUBLIN
Three generations of the Veldhuizen family work together to create artisanal cheeses like Red Neck Cheddar, Greens Creek Gruyère, and Bosque Blue. Their herd are predominately Jerseys, which are known for rich, creamy milk. *VeldhuizenCheese.com*

FARMS

B & G'S GARDEN, POOLVILLE
Though their specialty crops are Kiowa blackberries and two types of asparagus, this northern Parker County farm also grows many other varieties of elite-quality produce. Look for B & G master gardener Ben Walker and co-owner Greg Johnson at the Cowtown Farmers Market. *BandGGarden.com*

COLD SPRINGS FARM, WEATHERFORD
Using sustainable practices, Beverly Thomas grows rare and heirloom vegetables, fruits, herbs, and flowers, and her CSA members are frequently treated to fascinating varieties. For the person who has everything, check out her gift boxes of sweet potatoes, beans, veggies, and honey. *ColdSpringsFarmCSA.com*

EDEN'S ORGANIC GARDEN CENTER AND CSA FARM, BALCH SPRINGS
Marie Tedei's fourteen-acre urban farm, just twenty minutes from downtown Dallas, maintains a strong outreach program to educate the community on the benefits of sustainable farming. *EdensOrganicFarm.com*

FM 1410, DALLAS
For more than twenty years, urban farmer and produce broker Tom Spicer has been on the leading edge of the Dallas food movement. And the Spiceman is still the go-to guy for specialty produce. Look for him on Facebook or at his East Dallas shop. *1410 North Fitzhugh Avenue, Dallas, TX 75204*

FULL QUIVER FARMS, KEMP
The mission of Michael and Debbie Sams's family farm is to produce fresh, wholesome food using sustainable, organic practices. They raise Jersey and Holstein cows for their dairy products and their pigs feed on the whey from their cheese-making process. *FullQuiverFarmTX.com*

GREER FARM, DAINGERFIELD
At this rural haven in East Texas, you can rent a log cabin, pick your own blueberries, blackberries, figs, and plums, and take cooking classes with Eva. Sid Greer also raises grass-finished Maine-Anjou cattle. *GreerFarm.com*

LARKEN FARMS, WAXAHACHIE
Larken Farms has more than seven thousand trees with thirty-nine varieties of peaches, pears, and blackberries. Though not certified, owners Kent and Laura Jo Halverson practice organic methods. *LarkenFarms.com*

LEMLEY'S PRODUCE AND PLANT FARM, CANTON
An iconic figure at the Dallas Farmers Market, Mr. J.T. Lemley has been selling his tomatoes and Eight-Ball squash there for thirty-five years. Look for him on Facebook. *(903) 848-9411*

TASSIONE FARMS, STEPHENVILLE
Since 1997, Rocky and Celeste Tassione have provided locally grown organic baby lettuces, vegetables, and herbs to Dallas and Fort Worth restaurants. Follow them on Facebook. *(940) 769-2421*

MEAT AND SEAFOOD

BROKEN ARROW RANCH, INGRAM
Hill Country purveyors of wild game, the Hughes family ships USDA-inspected meat to cooks and professional chefs around the world. Their free-range venison, antelope, and wild boar are humanely harvested from more than a million acres of Texas ranchlands and field dressed in a high-tech mobile processing unit. *BrokenArrowRanch.com*

BURGUNDY PASTURE BEEF, GRANDVIEW
Jon and Wendy Taggart's grass-finished beef is naturally raised on lush North Texas pastures. In their butcher shop, meat is dry aged, custom cut, and packaged after receiving USDA approval. They deliver in the Dallas–Fort Worth area or offer nationwide shipping. *BurgundyPastureBeef.com*

GENESIS BEEF, MCKINNEY
This high-quality, grass-fed beef is dry aged, custom cut, and packaged by a local artisan butcher. Matt and Heather Hamilton also own the Local Yocal Farm to Market. *GenesisBeef.com*

JUHA RANCH, BARRY
Operated by Judi Glasgow and Harry and Heath Butaud, JuHa produces grass-fed beef, lamb, pastured poultry and pork, ranch-raised rabbit, and fresh eggs. They also train and raise working ranch dogs. *JuHaCattleCompany.com*

REHOBOTH RANCH, GREENVILLE
The animals at the Hutchins family farm are raised on a natural diet in a natural environment. They offer grass-fed beef and lamb, pastured poultry and pork, Grade A raw goat's milk, and eggs from free-ranging hens. *RehobothRanch.com*

SLOANS CREEK FARM, DODD CITY
Nathan and Ellen Melson raise heritage livestock breeds on their sustainable family farm. They sell grass-fed beef, lamb, chevon, and pastured pork. *SloansCreekFarm.com*

TJ'S SEAFOOD MARKET, DALLAS
This fresh seafood market and catering company has been family owned since 1989. Jon Alexis provides land-locked Dallas with a diverse selection of seasonal and sustainably sourced fish. *TJsSeafood.com*

WINDY MEADOWS FAMILY FARMS, COMMERCE
Said to be the best-tasting chicken in North Texas, the Hale family pastured chicken frequently graces the tables of the area's finest restaurants. For twenty years, Mike and Connie Hale have responsibly raised chicken, beef, and lamb on their forty acres. *WindyMeadowsFamilyFarm.com*

MISCELLANEOUS

TEXAS OLIVE RANCH, CARRIZO SPRINGS
Near the Texas-Mexico border, the Texas Olive Ranch, with more than forty thousand olive trees, has been at the forefront of the state's burgeoning oil business. Owner Jim Henry offers eleven varieties of olive oils, including one infused with natural mesquite. *TexasOliveRanch.com*

LUSCOMBE FARM, ANNA

Leslie Luscombe's gourmet jalapeño jellies are made with fresh peppers, blackberries, and peaches from local farms. You can find her every Saturday during growing season at the McKinney Chestnut Square farmers' market. *LuscombeFarm.com*

TEXAS ORGANIC MUSHROOMS, DENISON

This family-owned organic shiitake mushroom farm is a favorite among the area's most renowned chefs. Grown in environmentally controlled growing rooms, the mushrooms are free from pests and chemicals and picked at peak of their freshness and flavor. *Shiitakes.com*

ORGANIC GARDENING

NORTH HAVEN GARDENS, DALLAS

This full-service garden center offers knowledgeable assistance and seasonal classes on the growing of organic vegetables and herbs. *NHG.com*

STORES WITH ARTISANAL FOOD PRODUCTS

PATINA GREEN HOME AND MARKET, MCKINNEY

On McKinney's central square, Patina Green stocks artisanal food products alongside vintage furniture and home accessories. Chef Robert Lyford's lunch menu is inspired by what's fresh at the local farmers' market. *PatinaGreen.typepad.com*

LOCAL YOCAL FARM TO MARKET, MCKINNEY

At this old-fashioned grocery, rancher Matt Hamilton sells his own grass-fed beef as well as the products of his fellow farmers, ranchers, and food artisans. Products include pasture-raised chicken, artisan cheese, organic milk, and seasonal produce. He also operates a full-service butcher shop. *LocalYocalFarmtoMarket.com*

BOLSA MERCADO, DALLAS

Bolsa Mercado, a gourmet market and eatery, is located in the Oak Cliff section of Dallas, just a few doors away from its sister restaurant Bolsa. Behind the market's 30-foot-long deli counter are house-made pastries and specialty meats, like duck confit and a prized collection of charcuterie. There's a juice and coffee bar, and a chalkboard menu offering daily-to-go options from chef Jeff Harris. In the grocery section, there's an abundance of farm eggs and dairy products, freshly picked produce, and handcrafted food specialties. The market's beer and wine selection features over 100 labels. *BolsaDallas.com*

CELEBRATION MARKET, DALLAS

Celebration Restaurant has been serving up home-cooked meals for forty years. Their adjacent market offers food to go as well as the products of Texas food artisans. *CelebrationRestaurant.com/market*

ELLERBE'S FINE FOODS, FORT WORTH

Molly McCook's farm-to-table restaurant also offers an alcove filled with specialty vinegars, jellies, olive oils, boutique wines, and handcrafted kitchen products. *EllerbeFineFoods.com*

SWEETS

DUDE, SWEET CHOCOLATE, DALLAS

This artisan chocolate shop is tucked among the revived vintage storefronts of Dallas's Bishop Arts District. Confectioner Katherine Clapner's innovative menu of chocolates and other sweets changes with the seasons. *DudeSweetChocolate.com*

PIECURIOUS, DALLAS

Piecurious pies are made from scratch and delivered to your door. Baker Kate Nelson uses seasonal ingredients to create her selections—some sweet, some savory—from old family recipes. *PieCuriousCatering.com*

SAVOY SORBET

Linn Madsen's herbal sorbets are hand-made from purified water, organically grown herbs, and dried spices. Her sorbet's soothing flavors include Spiced Wine, Cinnamon Apple Brandy, and Lemon Thyme Balm. It's a refreshing, dairy-free dessert. *SavoySorbet.com*

STIR CRAZY BAKED GOODS, FORT WORTH
This family-run business specializes in made-to-order baked items. The Werners use local and organic ingredients whenever possible and much of their packaging is recycled, recyclable, and compostable. *StirCrazyBakedGoods.com*

ZIP CODE HONEY, TEXAS HONEY BEE GUILD, DALLAS
Beekeepers Brandon and Susan Pollard maintain hives in twenty Dallas County zip codes. Proceeds from the sale of their Zip Code Honey fund the guild's educational programs. For best health benefits, they suggest eating honey harvested from the nearest zip code. Find them on Facebook and at local farmers' markets. *texashoneybeeguild@yahoo.com*

FARMERS' MARKETS

Below is a partial list of the numerous farmers' markets located in North Texas. Check individual listings for opening and closing dates and hours of operation. For a more comprehensive list, go to our website: *EdibleDFW.com.*

CELEBRATION FARMERS MARKET: *CelebrationRestaurant.com/farmersmarket*

COPPELL FARMERS MARKET: *CoppellFarmersMarket.org*

COWTOWN FARMERS MARKET: *CowtownFarmersMarket.com*

DALLAS FARMERS MARKET: *DallasFarmersMarket.org*

DOWNTOWN ARLINGTON FARMERS MARKET: *DowntownArlingtonFarmersMarket.com*

GRAND PRAIRIE FARMERS MARKET: *gptx.org/farmersmarket*

KELLER FARMERS MARKET: *KellerFarmersMarket.com*

MCKINNEY FARMERS MARKET: *ChestnutSquare.org/programs/farmers_market.asp*

WHITE ROCK LOCAL MARKET: *WhiteRockLocalMarket.com*

ACKNOWLEDGMENTS FROM TRACEY RYDER

Edible Communities would like to thank our cofounder, Carole Topalian, for braving the intense summer heat of Texas and the studio to create the wonderfully delicious photographs for this book. Your vision and talent make us all look better! We would also like to thank Nanci and Terri Taylor, publisher and editor of the *Edible Dallas & Fort Worth* magazine, for adding yet another project to your already overly busy schedule and for creating a truly wonderful community-based cookbook with us. To Elissa Altman—no amount of thanks will ever be enough—your ability to rope and wrestle a cookbook to the ground as well as any Texas cowpoke says it all! And to our tireless recipes testers, we send our heartfelt thanks to all of you who brought these dishes to life for us in the kitchen and studio.

We also thank our agent, Lisa Ekus, for her ongoing support for all things Edible. To the team at Sterling Publishing, we offer our deepest gratitude for doing your best to honor the Edible look and brand, especially Carlo DeVito, Diane Abrams, Chris Thompson, Leigh Ann Ambrosi, and Blanca Oliveri.

Community cookbooks of this kind are not solitary projects and we are honored to have worked with a team as talented as this one while bringing this book into the world.

ACKNOWLEDGMENTS FROM TERRI TAYLOR

It may take a village to raise a child, but it takes a village plus a small army to birth a community cookbook.

To the 100 plus North Texas chefs, home cooks, farmers, ranchers, food artisans, and journalists who submitted their recipes, this book is dedicated to you. Thank you for taking the time to contribute to this project. Your stories and recipes reflect the diversity of our community, and you have affirmed my appreciation for our region's rich food culture.

Thank you to Edible Communities founders, Tracey Ryder and Carole Topalian, whose vision made this cookbook and Edible's network of local food magazines a reality. Thank you for your guidance and for trusting me with this assignment. Carole's insightful photographs bring these recipes and our community to life. What a privilege it was to spend a week with her, crisscrossing North Texas as she captured the local scene. Though our trek took place during the hottest, driest days of summer, she never once lost her smile or contagious enthusiasm.

To my executive editor, the gifted food writer Elissa Altman, thank you for keeping me on schedule and for sharing your expertise on recipe writing, which turns out to be a lot harder than one would imagine. To *Edible Seattle* editor Jill Lightner, who'd just completed her own cookbook, thank you for your good cheer, for having my back, and for patiently walking me through the process.

I could not have finished this project without the generous support of two local writers. Veteran food journalist Kim Pierce of the *Dallas Morning News* contributed greatly to these pages. She has been a champion of the local food scene for several decades, and for the last three years, she has unselfishly shared her knowledge with *Edible Dallas & Fort Worth*. Dallas food writer Kelly Yandell was my second angel. Kelly's passion for cooking and her good humor kept me sane. In the wee hours when deadlines were looming, these two women were always there to help with writing and research.

Edible Dallas & Fort Worth has an incredibly talented crew. Thanks to Debbie Bozeman, Steven Doyle, and Bari Henderson for gathering recipes. Thanks to journalists Teresa Gubbins and Danny Fulgencio for lending me their words. Thanks to copy editor Vivian Jones for keeping my commas in place and for always being a good listener. Thanks to gifted photographer and copy editor Matt Rainwater for being our Fort Worth bureau chief and for making me laugh. Thanks to our magazine's inventive layout designer Sergio Salvador for giving us artistic vision, and to Mary Ogle for translating that to the Internet. Thanks to Greg Jacob for moving mountains of magazines and to farmer Marie Tedei for keeping us in season. Thanks to Edible Communities' Kelly Day for cheerfully unraveling our paperwork. To every writer and photographer who has contributed to our magazine, thank you for all your hard work. You make my job a pleasure.

A whole new world opened up to me the day I began writing for *Edible Dallas & Fort Worth*. I owe a huge debt of gratitude to my sister, publisher Nanci Taylor, who has trusted me with the task of bringing her vision to the page. For three years, Nanci has worked tirelessly to promote our regional food producers and to make *Edible Dallas & Fort Worth* a success. This is her baby. If not for her blood, sweat, and dedication, our magazine and this cookbook would not exist. Thank you, Nanci, for giving me this tremendous opportunity.

Nanci and I would like to express our deepest gratitude to our parents John and Gloria Taylor, who taught us to laugh while we eat, and to our children, Kate, Matt, Trey, and Taylor, who have given us so much joy. To my husband Greg Mider, I couldn't have gotten through this whirlwind project without your love and encouragement. Thanks to the many friends who have supported *Edible Dallas & Fort Worth* since its inception. This book belongs to all of us. Thanks to the entire tribe.

168

INDEX